International Conference of LIGS University

Digital DataDriven Economy

Digital DataDriven Economy
The online conference June 28th29th, 2021
Editors:
PhDr. Peter Jan Kosmály, PhD. Dr. S
Suresh Kumar
Roman Lindauer, Dipl. Mgmt
Publisher:

1st Edition
ISBN: 978-0-9996639-0-5

Reference:
Kosmaly, P. J., Kumar, S. & Lindauer, R. (Eds.). (2021). Digital Data-Driven Economy. LIGS University. ISBN: 978-0-9996639-0-5

Partner

EDU Effective
MBA, LL.M., DBA

EDU Effective is a **nonprofit** educational institution established by the law of the Czech Republic, European Union, that offers **professional, highly practical and uptodate online education**, where you can learn from the **best leaders** in the industry, in **flexible 15 min classes** and gain a clear understanding of business to boost your professional career, launch, or scale your own business.

President's Message

Dear conference presenters, attendees and readers of the conference proceedings,

It was a great honor to meet all of you in the online space we created. The team of LIGS University spent many months preparing this event for not only our students but also everyone who wanted to join the panel discussion in Digital Business, Data Science, and new approaches in Economy and its digitalization.

I'm proud of my team as they managed to create a platform for sharing knowledge and experience with professionals from around the world.

As the theme of digitalization drives society forward, we could see many of you joining discussions and being very active. All presentations were professionally composed and backed up with solid research. We had overall 11 speakers from 6 countries attending. It is my pleasure to praise all facilitators and speakers for their professionalism and precise performance.

All attendees contributed to a very active audience. Many compelling discussions continued even after the presentation itself. I'm happy to say that the debates were fruitful and inspiring.

The overall atmosphere was friendly but still professional. I'm sure many of you made meaningful business connections that will be handy in the future. I can only hope all our future events will keep up the professionalism and keep getting even better.

Thank you, everyone, for your enthusiasm and efforts for this conference, and I look forward to upcoming online projects ahead.

Dr. Pavel Makovsky

LIGS University President

Table of Contents

President´s Message...5
Pavel Makovský

Quo Vadis Education in the Digital Age?...9
Peter Jan Kosmály

COVID 19 and Impact on Online Delivery..16
Jiri Medlen

The Impact of COVID 19 on Vietnam's Economy......................41
Liem Bui Quoc

Comparative Analysis of Integrated Marketing Communication...60
Jason Lee Carter

Exponential Growth in Corporate Innovation: A Synergy of Big Data, Cloud Computing & Digital Technologies...........................117
Deepak Kumar Dash

Big Data for Small and Mediumsized Enterprises..................152
Joy Weigand

The Effect of Technological Changes on Women's Entrepreneurial Behavior..175
Doris IkeOkereke

How Synergy of Economics Skills and Educational Methodology Help Transforming through the Communication Crisis and Beyond **198**
Vladimir Biruk

How Technological Changes Affect Human Behavior **228**
Adedayo Adetayo

How Technological Changes Affect Human Behavior **242**
Nnenna Uboma

How Technological Changes Affect Human Behavior **263**
Laura McCoy

Digital Dataware House (ETL) Transformation and its Cashless Economy **282**
Aslam Mohamed

Implications of Digital Technologies for Healthcare and Human Behavior **302**
Adinet Lock

Quo Vadis Education in the Digital Age? (opening speech)

Peter Jan Kosmály

Dear colleagues and participants of the Digital DataDriven Economy Conference! As an Academic Committee Chairperson I would like to welcome you and thank you for your contributions and your time.

As the topic and the environment of this conference are digital and its organizer is LIGS University, an online educational platform, please, let me present some thoughts on education in the digital age.

In recent decades the word "digital" became more and more popular and so did technologies, virtual environments, simulations, and so on. The word digital is derived from Latin digitus, meaning finger or toe – which can be used also as measuring instruments. Numbers under ten were counted on fingers long before today´s "digital age". Digital, thus, means finite; discrete, and analogue means continuous. As for the opposition of digital and analogue in the 20th century, it arose from the opposition of mechanical and technological instruments and various obtained results... Therefore, we can refer to the digital age or digital environment and think of the opposite of analogue, or we can simply refer to the actual state of society (humanity) and try to understand it.

In some cases the digital instrument has already lost its balance with its opposite and has become dominant – for example: "Who is interested in analogue TV broadcasting, when everyone uses the digital one?" The history of technologies facilitating and helping education is a history of modern humans, let´s use for a while the term homo sapiens. And let´s call the facilitating and helping tools –media. Let´s take a brief look on the question how digitalization of communication channels and media could be understood and how education could solve the tension between humans and the media humans use – but don´t want to be abused by them.

In the world of wikipedias, shared knowledge and a common knowledge base such as the Internet, a reception instruction (instructor) is essential for a proper use of obtained knowledge. Obviously, this is the essence of education – the relation between the educator, the educated one and the transferred knowledge. Evolution of education exploiting new technologies such as the Internet – started with distance learning using correspondence, television and other distant methods. A pioneer in this field was the Open University. The electronic education has brought the use of the Internet into consideration, firstly in the form of email discussions and public forums and later in the form of using computer programs facilitating the education. An example of an electronic education system is the learning management system Moodle. The modern age of the online education begins when those instruments of electronic education are fully used and reused in the online environment, basically without any limitations. This is when massive open online courses have stared somewhere around 2012 and so did one of the MOOC biggest projects – Coursera. So where are we nowadays?
This question does not deal only with knowledge and education, but also with media as instruments. Let´s take a brief look at Internet as a medium. Let´s consider medium a tool improving competencies and skills or facilitating education, and so on. Let´s consider the Internet not only a medium, but also a specific social formation using (and creating) own media and own social networks. Let´s look into the evolution of a medium in a nutshell on the example of the Internet. Let´s consider a mediaanthropological view and look at the relation of sapiens and digitalis.

We can call the first stage of the reception of media the extension, as it was explained by the famous media philosopher Mashall McLuhan. The newborn medium brings new opportunities, assistance, benefits, and facilitation. These were the times of email discussions, forums, first web pages and first search engines – catalogues. The second of four reception stages is the fascination, where the extent of possibilities outreaches the needs of the user and the user creates new needs and new media to

satisfy them. This is the period of the first social networks allowing sharing of files, music and later videos. The third stage is the narcosis when the medium and the needs created by using it start to dominate over the user. This is the example of social networks used as dopamine farms or virtual life platforms. The last and the fourth stage is the amputation (McLuhan´s term), or the necrosis, when originally extended competences and skills are lost in favor of the dependence on media. This is the state when socalled smartphones are raising children instead of their biological parents. Homo sapiens was replaced by homo digitalis.
We can see that media can be understood as:

- physical and tangible objects
- technical machines and appliances
- semiotic objects
- language or ideological constructs

Each type of those understandings has its own research and researchers. For example, media archeology studies unused, decommissioned, and so called "dead media". Great semiologists such as Ferdinand de Saussure, Charles Sanders Peirce, Roman Jakobson or Umberto Eco, studied the connection between language, symbols and symbolic systems. Others, such as Roland Barthes, Jean Baudrillard, the above mentioned Marshall McLuhan or the Czech media philosopher Vilém Flusser, contributed to the study of media with the terms exnomination as a secondary signification (Barthes); simulation and simulacra as hypersigns in hyperreality (Baudrillard); global village, global theater and media as extensions, messages (McLuhan), or technological images coded within a two dimensional reality and manifested in colors and surfaces (Flusser).
With every technological evolution we as humans go through, the need for ethical and educational revolutions becomes more and more obvious. Unethical and disproportionate use of media leads to reception defects, abuse of media and addictions. False projections give the idea that the connection of physical or symbolical instruments with human abilities creates a superficial being with the greatest abilities ever. This is of

course not true, because not only the Internet as a social formation, but also the education itself are a matter of cooperation. Cooperation is a healthy relation of dependence and independence. To find that right, healthful, and ethical relation we need to go back to the roots. To think analogically in the digital age and to use all the helpful instruments, but not to forget that the education is based on the triangle of the educator, the student and the knowledge. Therefore, to work constantly on improving the desirable skills, seek for the most helpful knowledge and to understand the student and his/her needs. It is great that here, in this digital environment, we can meet today and share our knowledge, raise research questions and seek for answers. I am very happy to be the human standing behind my electronic device and being ready to understand my fellow human beings with the help of the Internet, social networks and technologies.

Dear colleagues and participants, once again, welcome to the Digital Data Driven Economy Conference!

COVID19 and Impact on Online Delivery

Jiri Medlen

Abstract

The aim of the study is Coronavirus disease 2019 (COVID19) and the impact on ecommerce, specifically on online delivery. It compares e commerce Amazon and traditional companies Target, Walmart, and BestBuy before and after Christmas. The study's primary purpose is to show the significant dependency of companies like BestBuy on thirdparty services like UPS, USPS, and FedEx. The data is quite limited, so the author used a survey (50 surveyees via SurveyMonkey author's personal network), an interview (15 participants from the author's private network), and finally ran 2 natural experiments to measure the arrival time. Due to the high price of the item purchased (new iPad, Apple Pencil, Glass Screen Protector, and Smart Keyboard) and iWatch 6, the investigation is limited to Amazon, Target, Walmart, and BestBuy. The delivery item choice would affect the delivery time, so the iPad + accessories and iWatch 6 were chosen, and the author verified that the item is available. Amazon was able to deliver the complete set in 5 days. BestBuy was able to send the entire collection in 21 days. Amazon Prime is a significant advantage. However, if the item is in the store and the price is competitive, the buyer would most likely use an instore pickup.

Keywords: Amazon, BestBuy, COVID19, onlinedelivery

JEL Classification: D12, D30, D39

Introduction

COVID19 was first discovered in December 2019 in the "wet market" in Wuhan, province Hubei China. January 23, 2020, Wuhan was locked down at 10 AM (Yuan et al., 2020). It is not the first time. In 2003, Severe Acute Respiratory Syndrome (SARS) had emerged from China (Wiki,

2021m). Germany, Spain, Italy, France, and the rest of the EU are locking down all economic activities, education, and transport.

The US responded on January 31, 2020, with Coronavirus travel bans (Trump Proclamation 9984). March 13, 2020, after seeing an increase in COVID19 cases, Trump declares a National Emergency (Staff, 2021) and travel ban on NonUS citizens. The leader in responding to the virus's spread was California. March 19, an Executive "Stay at home Order" N33-20 was issued by California governor Newsom (Newsom, 2020; Staff, 2021). Other states followed very quickly after. By the end of March, approximately "316 mil. people (Mervosh et al., 2020) were ordered to stay home". March 27, Trump signs the CARES (The Coronavirus Aid, Relief, and Economic Security) Act into law (Wiki, 2021n).

Some industries like airlines, entertainment, travel, and hotels have been badly affected by the lockdown. Schools and nonessential businesses are closed. Joblessness in the USA (United States of America) went from 3.5% in Feb. 14.7% in Apr 2020 (Statista, 2021).

From the government perspective. One and only one solution is to vaccinate ~70 80% of the population and achieving herd immunity (one year to complete). March 11, 2021, Joe Biden signs a $1.9 trillion stimulus package (Pramuk, 2021) in the US to avoid layoffs from affected industries. Next is to pass a ~$2 trillion infrastructure bill to boost the economy.

From the US citizen perspective. How can people purchase cloth, electronics, etc., if all nonessential businesses are closed? Where is my stimulus check? How can people escape from the boring lockdown?

However, one element is very different from the past. After the Internet was invented, new companies like Amazon, Netflix, and ecommerce were born. This is offering an excellent alternative for shopping. Another interesting side effect of COVID19 and how hard lockdown can be on human psychology. People are trying to escape, but how? Theaters and concerts are closed. Netflix, Inc. (Walsh, 2020) added approximately15 mil. customers in the first couple of months of the COVID19 lockdown. The video game industry is another winner and sees an approximately 35% year over year increase (Smith, 2020) despite supply chain issues (Falk, 2020). Microsoft Xbox, Nintendo, and PS5 (Sony PlayStation 5) are the clear champions. People are looking for video games and entertainment to balance the lockdown.

The study's objective is to investigate the effect of the COVID19 on online delivery. The author is using multiple techniques to answer some of the complex questions. It is a mix of the Review of the Internet articles, Survey, Interview, and Experiments.

The Review of the Internet articles

The purpose is to generate primary data regarding ecommerce in general, in the US, and compare four major US companies Amazon, Target, Walmart, and Best Buy. Amazon starts from ecommerce, and the rest of the traditional companies has to penetrate ecommerce. What are the challenges COVID19 prepared for each of them? The author is trying to understand the delivery methods of each company. This will help to discover the reasons for late delivery.

Survey

The main reason to use a survey is to research a simple question: Did your Christmas gifts arrive on time (the US only)?

Interview

The interview is going to help with finding out what the reasons for late arrival are?

Research questions: Why Christmas gifts arrived late? What company did you use? Did you purchase an item instore or online?

Run two experiments

The purpose of the experiments is to see the performance of the four major companies Amazon, Target, Walmart, and Best Buy, in terms of online delivery of a couple of items iPad and iWatch 6. Measure time: How long does it take for the items to arrive?

Material and Methods

This section covers used methods and methodology.

Material:

Experiment 1: purchase a new iPad, Apple Pencil, Glass Screen Protector, Smart Keyboard online and measure arrival time (Amazon, BestBuy) at Christmas.

Experiment 2: purchase a new iWatch 6 online and measure arrival time (Amazon, Target, BestBuy, and Walmart) offseason (March).

Methods:

- Survey: Random sample of 50 participants from the author's personal network in the US (population = 473). The author is using quantitative statistical analysis for survey data analysis (Bhandari, 2020).

  • Interview: The interview was done for all participants who did not receive Christmas presents on time to understand the reasons (30% of respondents from the survey = 15 participants). Qualitative analysis thematic is employed to analyze unstructured text (interview).
- Experiment 1: Pick 4 items from the electronic category and verify availability instore and online.
- Experiment 2: Pick 1 item from the electronic category and verify availability instore and online. Note: Due to price, experiments 1 2 are limited.

Model and Data

This section covers used models and collected data.

Survey:

The author started with a simple survey (50 participants) to understand the following question limited to the US only: Did your Christmas gifts arrive on time (the US only)? The survey result shows that 70% of participants received their Christmas presents on time (for a baseline researcher applied 50%). The R script is prop.test(x = 35, n = 50, p = 0.5, correct = FALSE, alternative = "greater"). The result is significant (statistically) on a 95% level. Pvalue (Wiki, 2021a) = 0.002 and CI (Confidence interval) is in the range of (0.585, 1.000).

Interview:

The purpose is to find reasons for late delivery. 30% of respondents from the survey = 15 participants, unfortunately, did not receive Christmas presents on time. The interview will help determine the reasons for late and early arrival are.

Research question: Why Christmas gifts arrived late or early? Did you purchase an item instore or online? What company did you use?

Table 1. ***Provides Affinity Diagram Results for the Research Question: Why Christmas Gifts Arrived Late***

	Christmas gifts arrived late.	Christmas gifts arrived on time.
Reasons:	• Online purchases from BestBuy, Target, and Walmart (delivered by UPS, USPS, and FedEx). • Late purchase (less than 14 days) was 5 times. • Hot item purchase (PS5, Xbox) was ordered 3 times.	• Online purchase from Amazon; Pick up in-store Walmart, Target, BestBuy, and Costco. • Early purchase (four weeks).

Source: the Author

The interview revealed that some hot items like PS5 and Xbox did not arrive at all. The consequent analysis revealed that 72% of businesses suffered disruption in the supply chain (COVID19 disruption, 2020). **COVID19 has disrupted the supply chain** in a significant way. Companies did not diversify their supply chain portfolio. Foxconn could not deliver PS5 consoles on time. COVID 19 has proven an unhealthy US and EU dependency on China.

Additionally, the interview revealed that popular items like Instant Pot, Gravity Blanket, Fitbit, Massagers, Moon Lamps, laptops, AirPods, iWatch, iPads, and iPhones arrived late when items were ordered online from Costco, BestBuy; Target, and Walmart. The consequent analysis revealed several reasons for late arrival. **COVID19 has disrupted warehouse fulfillment. COVID19 lockdown has dramatically increased demand for UPS, USPS, and FedEx services, and as a result, items were delivered very late compare to Amazon, which has its own fleet.**

The interview revealed that items like graphic cards Nvidia RTX 30703090 are not arriving at all or very late. Analysis has shown that there are several reasons for it. **COVID19 lockdown is responsible for rising of the gaming industry. COVID19 has disrupted China's**

manufacturing. Chip shortage due to globalwide shutdowns because of COVID19. Cryptomining (Bitcoin and Ethereum) using GPU (Molloy, 2021).

Literature review – Ecommerce acceleration

From the chart (Figure 1), it is clear that ecommerce was accelerated during COVID19. The reason is simple lockdown. Only essential businesses were opened (for example, grocery stores). The rest had to be ordered online. The consequence of this was a significant increase in acceptance of digital (cashless) payment methods and the rise of ecommerce.

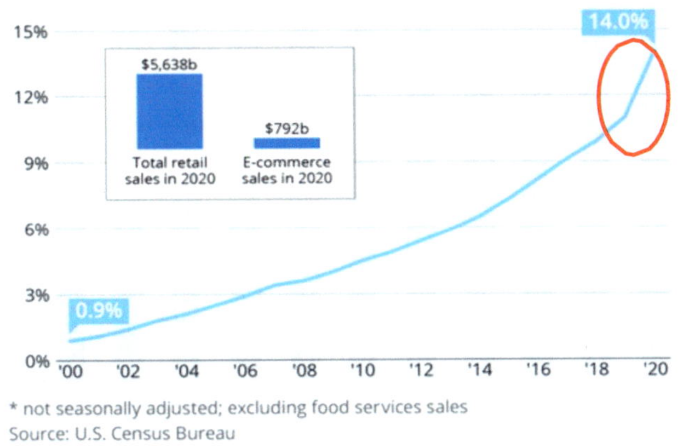

Figure 1. E commerce Sales as a % of Total Retail Sales in the US.

Source: Richter, 2021.

Literature review – Logistics

Data:	Amazon (Wiki, 2021d)	Target (Wiki, 2021c)	BestBuy (Wiki, 2021b)	Walmart (Wiki, 2001)
Year founded:	1996	1902	1966	1962
Employees 2020:	1,298,000	368,000	102,000	2,200,000
Revenue 2020:	$386 billion	$75 billion	43 billion	$559 billion
# of stores:	0 originally	1,900	977	11,443
Logistics (delivery):	Same-day delivery. One-Day delivery. Click-to-door 2.2 days average. Carriers: FedEx, UPS, and USPS, and 50% is delivered by Amazon. Curbside pickup is limited for AMZN (groceries only for $119/year).	Same-day delivery (free $35+). Carriers: FedEx, UPS, and USPS. Curbside pickup.	Same-day delivery (Instacart). Next-day delivery. Carriers: FedEx, UPS, and USPS. Curbside pickup.	Same-day delivery. Next-day delivery (only in some areas free $35+). Express delivery (2-hours or less + $10 extra). Carriers: FedEx, UPS, and USPS. Curbside pickup.

Table 2. Provides Primary Data of Each Company (Amazon, Target, BestBuy, and Walmart)

Source: the Author

Table 2 is exploring delivery methods for all four companies. Amazon delivered 2.5 billion packages/year, and in 2019 50% of its packages (BLANCO, 2019). Amazon is becoming the largest package deliverer in the US. Amazon fleet has 80 planes, over 30k branded vans, 20k trailers, and 800 Amazon Delivery Partners with 75k drivers in the US. Projection is 3.5 billion packages/year (BLANCO, 2019). Amazon's average clicktodoor time is 2.2 days, in contrast with the industry standard of 5.1 days. After COVID19, Amazon expects a volume drop.

Target, BestBuy, and Walmart are using carriers: FedEx, UPS, and USPS and, therefore, sometimes cannot deliver on time.

Literature review – Supply Chain:

The purpose is to find COVID19 related reasons for late delivery.

COVID19 has disrupted the supply chain, and 72% of businesses suffered disruption in the supply chain (COVID19 disruption, 2020).

Lockdown is hard on human psychology. Ettman et al. (2020) argued that the "depression in the US had increased more than 3fold during COVID 19." People are looking for video games and entertainment to balance the lockdown. The video game industry sees an approximately 35% year over year increase (Smith, 2020) despite supply chain issues. Table 3 is answering some essential questions regarding the supply chain and COVID19 impact.

Table 3. *Provides Supply Chain Analysis*

Supply chain:		
Element1:	Purpose:	To understand the reasons why some items were so late.
	Research question:	Why were some items late and even Amazon could not deliver? Specifically, PS5.
	Result:	72% of businesses suffered disruption in the supply chain (COVID-19 disruption, 2020). • PS5 is manufactured in Foxconn China Shenzhen facility, and due to COVID-19 lockdown, Foxconn could deliver 50% of PS5 consoles for Christmas (Mochizuki & Wu, 2020). • At the same time, demand spiked around 35% for games (Smith, 2020).
	Conclusion:	**COVID-19 has disrupted the supply chain** in a significant way. Companies did not diversify their supply chain. Foxconn could deliver PS5 consoles on time.
	Solution:	• Sony is planning nearly all-automated factories in Japan (Writer, 2020) to combat supply chain disruption. • Diversification of the supply chain.
Element2:	Research question:	Did the COVID-19 pandemic affect fulfillment in warehouses?

	Result:	• Amazon 20k workers infected by COVID-19 (BBC News, 2020).
		Amazon has approximately 1.13 million employees, which equals 1.7% of employees are infected by COVID-19.
		• USPS 7.4k infected (USPS, 2021a).
		• The assumption is that it is similar for USPS and FedEx. The reason is simple:
		  • No vaccination.
		  • N-95 masks and PPE are only available for frontline workers (hospitals).
		Note: China cannot produce N-95 masks, and 70% of N-95s from China fail quality tests (Brooks, 2020).

	Conclusion:	Yes, the COVID-19 pandemic has negatively affected fulfillment in warehouses, and this would **affect item shipping**. However, it would be hard to measure the delay because of other factors.
	Solution:	Vaccination and N-95 masks + PPE (US government has to implement re-shoring and near-shoring in strategic areas).
Element3:	Research question:	Was there a volume spike due to the COVID-19 pandemic in shipments?
	Result:	• Amazon 49% increase (Mattioli, 2020). • USPS 25% increase (USPS, 2021). • UPS 21% increase (Ziobro, 2020). • FedEx 21% increase (Risher, 2020).
	Conclusion:	Yes, there was a significant volume spike in shipments. COVID-19 lockdown is forcing people to purchase online, and as a result, USPS, UPS, and FedEx see a considerable spike in volumes, and **delivery is late**. As a result, e-commerce was accelerated during COVID-19.
	Solution:	• Warehouse automation. • Companies like Walmart, Target, and BestBuy have to maybe invest in their own fleet.

Source: the Author

Experiment 1:

The purpose of Experiment 1 is to compare online purchases and compare the shopping experience. Due to the high price, this is limited to only BestBuy and Amazon. The price was identical in both stores. A simple purchase of a new iPad, Apple Pencil, Glass Screen Protector, Smart Keyboard online and measure arrival time.

Table 4. ***Provides Comparison Online for Amazon and BestBuy (Purchase of a New iPad, Apple Pencil, Glass Screen Protector, and Smart Keyboard)***

Date:	BestBuy	Amazon	Notes:
12/1/2020	Order.	Order.	
12/2/2020	Pencil – shipped.		
12/2/2020	Glass Screen Protector – shipped.		
12/4/2020	iPad - Smart Keyboard – shipped.		
12/5/2020		**Delivered All 4.**	All four items - **delivered.**
12/6/2020	Pencil – late.		Carrier estimate 12/11.
12/9/2020	iPad – late.		Carrier estimate 12/10.
12/10/2020	Pencil – **delivered.**		
12/10/2020	iPad – **delivered.**		
12/17/2020	Smart Keyboard.		Price Adjustment.
12/19/2020	Smart Keyboard – **delivered.**		
12/21/2020	Glass Screen Protector – **delivered.**		
12/24/2020	**Christmas.**		**Amazon is 4x faster.**

Source: the author

Conclusion: Amazon was able to deliver all items in 5 days Amazon Prime. BestBuy in 21 days (UPS could not handle the load).

Experiment 2:

Keep in mind that the Christmas season is the busiest, so to compensate for it, let's purchase iWatch 6 from Amazon, Target, BestBuy, and Walmart in March and measure delivery time.

Table 5.
Comparison Online

		Amazon	Target	BestBuy	Walmart
In-store:	Available	NA	YES	YES	YES
Online:	Available	YES	YES	YES	YES
	Price	$349	$399	$349	$349
	Ordered	March 13	March 13	March 13	March 13
	Delivered	March 15	March 17	March 15	March 17

for Amazon, Target, BestBuy, and Walmart (Purchase of a New iWatch 6)

Conclusion: Amazon and BestBuy were able to deliver all items in 3 days. Target and Walmart in 5 days. However, the purchaser can immediately pick up the item instore (except Amazon), and Amazon, BestBuy, and Walmart have the same price, $349, and Target would match the price. So, Amazon might not have an advantage with fast delivery.

Results and Discussion

This section sums up the results and continues with a discussion. The paper talks about the COVID19 and the impact on online delivery. From the data Figure 1, it is visible that ecommerce has accelerated. The main reason is simple. Nonessential businesses are closed due to COVID19, and the only way to order anything is online. The survey revealed that 30% of Christmas presents were late. The interview and consequent analysis revealed the main reasons for late delivery. **COVID19 has disrupted the supply chain and, at the same time, showing an unhealthy US and EU dependency on China.** If the supply chain was correctly done with a healthy mix of reshoring, nearshoring, and offshoring, the disruption would have been relatively small. Significant reasons were supply chain disruption for some hot items like (PS5, Xbox). COVID19 has disrupted warehouse fulfillment. **COVID19 lockdown has dramatically increased demand for UPS, USPS, and FedEx services, and as a result, items were delivered very late compare to Amazon, which has its own fleet.** UPS, USPS, and FedEx could not handle the massive increase in online orders and COVID19. A large number of employees contracted COVID19 in warehouses, and this impacted doortodoor delivery as well. There is another reason for some items like graphic cards Nvidia RTX 30703090 not being delivered. **Cryptomining (Bitcoin and Ethereum) using GPU** (Molloy, 2021). Today we are experiencing an SSD (solidstate drive) shortage, and the reason is **cryptomining (Chia)**. What are the solutions? **Balanced supply chain, warehouse automation, automated factories, and autonomous delivery. In other words, remove humans from the working process using fully automated solutions. Ecofriendly cryptomining.**

Experiment 1 and 2 confirmed that Amazon due to it private fleet was able to handle the load. The question is, should Walmart, Target, and BestBuy build their own private fleet? It is costly.

Conclusion

This section covers the most critical points of the study.

Table 6. *Provides Final Conclusions*

Conclusion:	There is strong evidence that COVID-19 has impacted online delivery.
	• In early-stage, some hot items like PS5 could not be **delivered at all** due to China's lockdown and **supply chain breakdown.**
	• COVID-19 lockdown is forcing people to order online, and as a result carrier: FedEx, UPS, and USPS see a significant spike in delivery, and **delivery is late.**
	• **Crypto-mining.**
	• There is evidence that COVID-19 has impacted fulfillment in:
	  • Warehouses of Amazon, Target, BestBuy, and Walmart.
	  • Carriers: FedEx, UPS, and USPS.
	And as a result, it **affected online delivery**.
	Supply Chain:
	• COVID-19 has disrupted the supply chain and has exposed our dependency on China and India.
	• COVID-19 has impacted warehouse fulfillment.
	Delivery Fleets:
	• COVID-19 has impacted the delivery fleet of FedEx, UPS, and USPS.
	• COVID-19 has affected warehouse fulfillment of FedEx, UPS, and USPS.
	COVID-19 has negatively impacted the time of the delivery.

Recommendation:	Supply Chain: • It is crucial to implement re-shoring and near-shoring to minimize dependency on China and India. SP5, N-95 masks, and medicine are classic examples of such a dependency. In some cases, like medicine, it is life-threatening (however, the government has to step in). • The second important factor is to develop nearly all-automated factories. This will limit pandemic exposure on workers. • The third important factor is warehouse automation. This will limit pandemic exposure on workers. • The fourth important factor is a good supply of N-95 masks and PPEs to limit pandemic exposure on workers and limit liability. Delivery Fleets: • It is not necessary for Walmart, BestBuy, and Target to build a massive delivery fleet like Amazon because they have an ample number of stores. Customers can easily pick up in-store if the price is competitive. • The limited delivery fleet would be helpful for customers far away from the store's proximity. • It is vital to watch Amazon closely and see how many stores they have, and adjust the strategy accordingly. • Uber/Lift could help in some instances. Self-driving cars and drone delivery might help in the future.

Source: the Author

References and bibliography

Citation of websites

1. BBC News. (2020, October 2). Nearly 20,000 Covid19 cases among Amazon workers. https://www.bbc.com/news/business54381928

2. Bhandari, P. (2020, July 3). A stepbystep guide to data collection. https://www.scribbr.com/methodology/datacollection/ https://www.scribbr.com/category/methodology/#examplesofdata-collection methods

3. BLANCO, S. (2019, December 20). Amazon Buying So Many Commercial Vans, It's a Boom for Mercedes, FCA, and Ford. https://www.caranddriver.com/news/a30295937/amazoncommercial-vansford mercedesfca/

4. Ettman, C. K., Adballa, S. M., Cohen, G. H., MPhil, M. S. W., Sampson, L., Vivier, P. M., & Galea, S. (2020, September 2). Prevalence of depression symptoms in us adults before and during the COVID19 pandemic.

5. Falk, J. (2020, April 27). US must reduce dependence on China dominated supply chains, says Baker Institute report. https://news.rice.edu/ 2020/04/27/usmustreducedependenceonchina-dominatedsupply chainssaysbakerinstitutereport2/

6. Mattioli, D., & Herrera, S. (2020, May 1). Amazon's Sales Jump as Coronavirus Prompts Surge in Online Shopping. https://www.wsj.com/ articles/amazonssalesjumpascoronavirus-promptssurgeinonline shopping11588278740

7. Mervosh, S., Lu, D., & Swales, V. (2020, April 20). See which states and cities have told residents to stay at home. The New York Times. https://www.nytimes.com/interactive/2020/us/coronavirusstayat-home order.html

8. Mochizuki, Wu, T. D. (2020, September 14). Sony Cuts PlayStation 5 Forecast by 4 Million https://www.bloomberg.com/tosv2.html? vid=&uuid=c00456f0-

a22d11ebb858
b333f1046bab&url=L25ld3MvYXJ0aWNsZXMvMjAyMC0wOS0xNS9zb255LWI
zLXNhaWQtdG8tY3V0LXBzNS1mb3JlY2FzdC1ieS00LW1pbGxpb24tZHVlLXRv
LWNoaXAtd29lcw==
9. Molloy, B. D. (2021, January 24). The great graphics card shortage of 2020

(and 2021). Retrieved January 1, 2021, from https://www.bbc.com/news/ technology-55755820

10. Newsom, G. (2020, March 19). Executive Order N-33-20. Executive department state of California. https://www.gov.ca.gov/wp-content/uploads/ 2020/03/3.19.20-attested-EO-N-33-20-COVID-19-HEALTH-ORDER.pdf

11. Pramuk, J. (2021, March 11). Biden signs $1.9 trillion Covid relief bill, clearing way for stimulus checks, vaccine aid. https://www.cnbc.com/ 2021/03/11/biden-1point9-trillion-covid-relief-package-thursday- afternoon.html

12. Redman 1, R. (2021, March 11). Report: Amazon has 28 more Amazon Fresh stores in the works. https://www.supermarketnews.com/retail-financial/ report-amazon-has-28-more-amazon-fresh-stores-works

13. Richter, F. (2021, February 24). Pandemic Accelerates Shift to Online Retail. https://www.statista.com/chart/14011/e-commerce-share-of-total- retail-sales/

14. Risher, W. (2020, December 1). FedEx kicks into high gear as the peak holiday season arrives. https://dailymemphian.com/article/18397/fedex-kicks-into-high-gear-as-peak-season-arrives

15. Smith, N. (2020, May 12). The giants of the video game industry have thrived in the pandemic. Can the success continue? https:// www.washingtonpost.com/video-games/2020/05/12/video-game-industry-coronavirus/

16. Staff, A. (2021, January 1). A Timeline of COVID-19 Developments in 2020.
https://www.ajmc.com/view/a-timeline-of-covid19-developments-in-2020

17. Statista (2021, February 11) U.S. unemployment rate: seasonally adjusted.
https://www.statista.com/statistics/273909/seasonally-adjusted- monthly-unemployment-rate-in-the-us/

18. USPS (2021, January 1). https://about.usps.com/newsroom/national-releases/2021/0209-usps-reports-first-quarter-fiscal-2021-results.htm#:~:text=Meanwhile%2C%20the%20Postal%20Service's%20sales,by%20the%20surge%20in%20e%2D

19. USPS. (2021a, November 20). https://www.uspsoig.gov/document/ employee-safety-%E2%80%93-postal-service-covid-19-response

20. Walsh, J. (2020, October 21). Netflix Subscriber Growth Slows After Surging During Pandemic.

https://www.forbes.com/sites/joewalsh/ 2020/10/20/netflix-subscriber-growth-slows-after-surging-during- pandemic/?sh=313bbc8e244e

21. Wiki. (2001, September 12). Walmart. https://en.wikipedia.org/wiki/ Walmart

22. Wiki. (2021a, February 6). P-value. https://en.wikipedia.org/wiki/P-value

23. Wiki. (2021b, March 12). Best Buy. https://en.wikipedia.org/wiki/ Best_Buy

24. Wiki. (2021c, March 12). Target Corporation. https://en.wikipedia.org/ wiki/Target_Corporation

25. Wiki (2021d, March 12). Amazon (company). https://en.wikipedia.org/ wiki/Amazon_(company)

26. Wiki (2021m, April 19). 2002–2004 SARS outbreak. https:// en.wikipedia.org/wiki/2002%E2%80%932004_SARS_outbreak

27. Wiki (2021n, April 16). CARES Act. https://en.wikipedia.org/wiki/ CARES_Act

28. Writer, S. (2020, July 4). PlayStation's secret weapon: a nearly all-automated factory. https://asia.nikkei.com/Business/Companies/ PlayStation-s-secret-weapon-a-nearly-all-automated-factory

29. Yuan, Z., Xiao, Y., Dai, Z., Huang, J., Zhang, Z., & Chen, Y. (2020). Modelling the effects of Wuhan's lockdown during COVID-19, China. Bulletin of the World Health Organization, 98(1), 484-494.

30. Ziobro, P. (2020, July 30). UPS Rides E-Commerce Surge to 21% Jump in Package Volumes. https://www.wsj.com/articles/ups-rides-e- commerce-surge-to-21-jump-in-package-volumes-11596105832#: %7E:text=UPS%20UPS%200.92%25%20said%20its,early%20days%20of %20the%20pandemic.

Contact information

Name of the author: Jiri Medlen

Affiliation (University): LIGS University student

Email: jiri.medlen@gmail.com

The Impact of COVID19 on Vietnam's Economy: Changes in Digital Communication

Liem, Bui Quoc

Abstract

COVID-19 pandemic has a huge impact on every sector and business of Vietnam's economy and during the health crisis, the economy has rapidly transformed digitally and most of businesses have made significant changes in digital marketing communications. Using statistical methods and comparison analysis, I analyzed all statistical data about digital communications in 2019 and in 2020, pre-crisis and during-crisis of coronavirus outbreak, and compare them to answer two questions: (1) the impacts of COVID-19 on Vietnam's economy in term of digital transformation, and (2) the changes of digital marketing communications that businesses have made.

COVID-19 has changed the national economy and boosted the digital transformation to provide the customers with better experiences in reducing contacts with others in social distancing.

Interaction between businesses and their customers are more based on artificial intelligence applications, blockchain and big data, digital communications, fintech and shipping services.

They have moved from web-based communications to more digital platforms as fan page, group page, chat applications and video contents.

Keywords: digital transformation, digital communications, digital platforms, COVID-19 epidemic

JEL Classification: M30, M37, M38

Introduction

In the COVID-19 interval, in Vietnam, everything has gone on-line and the rate of Internet uses has strongly increased. According to We are social,

64 million Vietnamese people use the Internet, 50 million people have more than one social media account and 70 million people have mobile devices (Tien et al. 2020). On average, the users spend more than 6 hours chatting, entertaining, doing business and surfing information. During the COVID-19 outbreak, traditional communication channels are not completely used as digital ones are more effective (Do et al. 2020). Technology 4.0 has brought the consumers to more online consumption, online education and online entertainment, requiring the businesses to adapt their communication campaigns to more digital approach.

In the times of social distancing, businesses work with customers via digital platforms to sell products though they work from home (Doan, 2020). With the shipping company as Grab, Gojek, Be, Now, Giaohangtietkiem..., the products are delivered to customers at low costs and businesses can increase the customers' habits of placing orders on-line. Therefore, there are changes in digital communication to focus on customers who work from home, purchase food and necessary things for their daily lives during lockdown and businesses also maintain sales revenues (Nguyen et al. 2020). COVID-19 outbreak has shaped a new economic image with more digital applications, affecting every resident who surfs the Internet to read communication content and every business which can improve its target achievement. Digital communication has become the most appropriate option for Vietnam's business world in particular and the whole country in general. The research will focus on the impact of COVID-19 on Vietnam's economy in terms of digital communication to see the increasing opportunities for businesses to strategically map out their marketing communication campaigns in a new era.

Literature review

COVID19 in Vietnam

Vietnam has remarked that the country is successful in dealing with the COVID-19 pandemic (Trevisan et al. 2020). Updated until May 2, 2021, the country has had 2,962 cases, in which 2,549 recovered and 35 died.

The bad experience in Wuhan, China in the early 2020 brought Vietnam's government's attention and they decided to cope with this challenge immediately with compulsory measures. The government required the Vietnamese to use a mobile app, called NCOVI, and a hotline for their health status and travel history declaration to find F0, F1, F2, F3, and F4 (Vietnam Times, 2020). These contacts are mapped and the people may be required to be quarantined or tracked down within 14 days in an isolated area or at home with strict supervision. The whole market receives negative impact with the closures of shopping malls, cinemas, bars and pubs, restaurants, schools..., pushing the digital communication transformation process when all everything turns online shopping and home delivery.

Digital communications in COVID19 era in Vietnam

As there are some areas in a city are socially quarantined and people are restricted or limited to leave their houses, businesses have no choices but make their websites and social media fan pages more interactive with their customers and create communication applications for them to download. The purposes of these channels are to maintain sales revenue by making online sales and managing customer relationships (Tien et al., 2021). Besides, the consumers staying home to work or entertain increase their more time to be on-line and this is an opportunity for businesses to boost their communication on advertising their brands digitally in diversified platforms as Facebook, Youtube, Twitter, Tiktok, Zalo and newly born applications. Digital communication, therefore, is a new but powerful trend in the COVID-19 era, supporting businesses to convey digital brand messages and improve their audio-visual designing competences to attract more viewers and make their brand stories viral (Hoang et al. 2021). Once outdoor activities are limited, people turn to the Internet to work and study, so brands can take advantages of new trends to earn sales as much as possible not only to survive but also catch up with the consumers' new habits in the new normal life. The development of e-commerce, cashless payment and Internet speed has shifted the online shopping into an indispensable demand.

There is a lack of research in examining the impact of COVID-19 on Vietnam's economy in terms of digital communication when businesses need to both save cost and optimize their communication budget in campaigns for increasing brand awareness and nurture Internet users for their brands. In terms of big data analytics from social media and the case study of Vietnam, this research aims to answer the following three questions:

RQ1: What are the impacts of COVID-19 on Vietnam's economy in term of digital transformation?

RQ2: To what extent businesses in Vietnam change and develop their digital communication campaigns?

Methodology

Statistical methods are used to compare the digital communications before and during the pandemic basing on the content delivered in different social media platforms popularly accessed in Vietnam, including Facebook, Zalo, Instagram and Tiktok. Besides, information sources are also collected from digital newspapers, forums and blogs to create a more complete picture of digital communications in the COVID-19 era. Decrease in sales in a lot of businesses and increase in other businesses show that small businesses are negatively impacted while others quickly digitalize their sales process and communications. Data for media are categorized into digital mainstream media and social media platforms as two main types of communication channels used in the outbreak. A comparison is made in pre-disease crisis and during-disease crisis to see changes in digital communications and how this impacts the sales of businesses trying to cope with the pandemic.

Results

The impact of COVID19 on Vietnam's economy

According to Tran et al. (2020), the outbreak has influenced the household income with 0.3% increase in income, 33% unchanged, and 72% decrease (figure 1). The economy also sees not many jobs created but the statistics show 9% workers fired, 31% workload reduction, 9% overtime work and 53% unchanged. People working in healthcare still maintain their stable incomes rather than other sectors as their workload increase or even work overtime to work with patients. For macroeconomic statistics, Vietnam's 2020 GDP increased by 2,9%, the lowest on record but still made high impression in comparison with other countries in the region. The economy witnessed a significant growth in many sectors as agriculture (2.7%), industrial and construction (4%), and retails and services (2.3%) thanks to good control over the disease in Vietnam (Timvest 2021). The outbreak has forced the government to impose nationwide lockdown, suspension of public transportation, at-home work, prohibition of cultural, sport and entertainment activities, the temporary closure of unessential business operations and travel bans. This has made online shopping, e- commerce and mobile payment increase with the development of sales application and websites.

Figure 1. ***Income Changes in COVID19 in Vietnam***

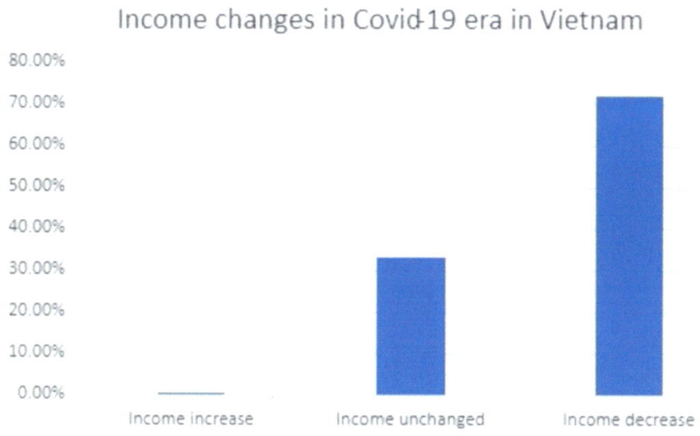

Source: Tran, B. X., Nguyen, H. T., Le, H. T., Latkin, C. A., Pham, H. Q., Vu, L. G., ... & Ho, R. C. (2020). Impact of COVID-19 on Economic Well-being and Quality of Life of the Vietnamese During the National Social Distancing. Frontiers in psychology, 11.

Digital communications in predisease era

With low-cost internet access and better high-speed connections, spending in mobile advertising has increased by 7.9 percent accounting for 67.1 percent of digital advertising revenue. Mobile users prefer using applications for social networking, chat and video entertainment, inspiring advertisers to communicate their brands on these applications besides other leading social media platforms as Facebook, Zalo, Youtube and

Tiktok (Statista, 2021). 71 percent of Gen Z and millennial users watch daily digital videos while 42 percent like to watch video streaming for at least two hours every day. Thanks to this, around 49 percent of business users apply their communication campaigns on social media and search engine from Google, Cốc Cốc and Safari (Cuong, 2019). From figure 2, there is an increase in advertising spending from 211.6 million U.S dollars in 2019 to 227.4 million in 2020 and the forecast is 242.2 in 2021. According to a statistic outcome, 40 percent of users watch the online advertising, click on the pop-up advertising and get willing to share if the content is appealing to them.

Figure 2. *Advertising Spending Since 2018 in Vietnam*

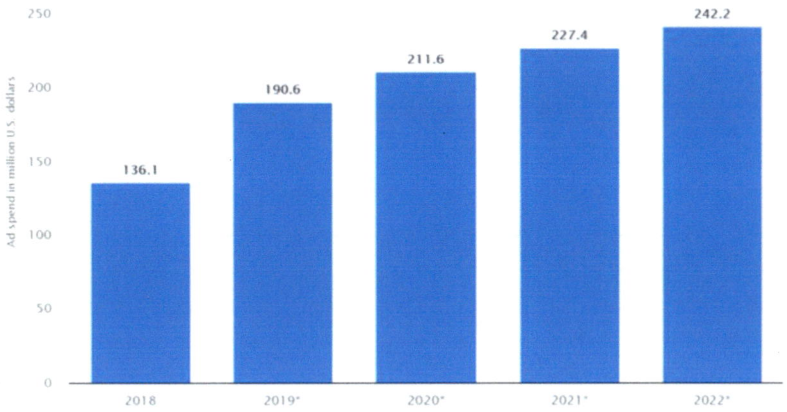

Source: Statista. (2020). Digital Advertising Expenditure Share of Total Media Advertising Expenditure in Vietnam in 2018 with Forecasts until 2022. Retrieved: 14 July 2021, from: https://www.statista.com/statistics/771572/digital-ad-spending- share-of-total-media-ad-spending-vietnam/

Digital communications in the COVID19 era

With the COVID-19 outbreak, Vietnamese users accessing information on-line and watching videos on social media has become increasingly trending in digital communications (AsiaPac, 2020). In comparison with the previous year, there is a 10% increase in Internet users, a 9.6% increase in social media users, and a 15% increase in watching online videos. Businesses invest more in writing and producing digital contents on social media, making these platforms as the mainstreams of digital communications (Le & Ratten, 2021). Facebook, Youtube, Zalo, Facebook Messengers, Instagram are the top five social media platforms with more digital contents created to increase brand awareness, sales activities, education, healthcare and entertainment (figure 3). The consumption rate of digital videos has attracted more engagement from the audience, increasing views, comments, shares and edits. There is also a significant increase in Tiktok influencers who produce humorous or meaningful digital content and then become brand ambassadors or brand communicators. These online influencers become a new choice for businesses to do co-branding with or cooperate in digital communications at low expenses.

Figure 3. *Mostused Social Media Platforms in Vietnam*

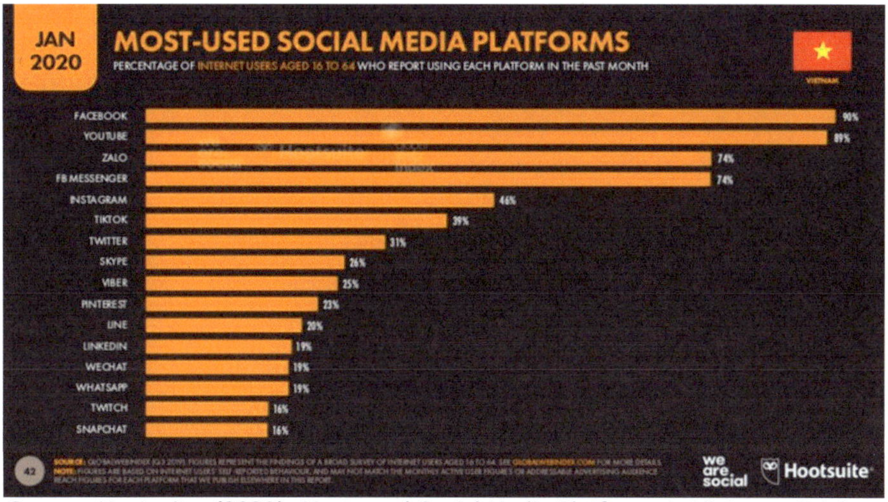

Source: Hootsuite. (2020). Most-used Social Media Platforms in Vietnam. Retrieved: 14 July 2021, from: https://www.hootsuite.com/resources/digital-2020

Discussion

Transformation of Vietnam's economy into more digital approaches

Both public and private businesses understand the importance of digital changes in their marketing communications to adapt the business processes to the "new normal". COVID-19 has quickly changed the national economy and boosted the digital transformation to provide the customers with better experiences in reducing contacts with others in social distancing (Nguyen et al., 2021). Interaction between businesses and their customers are more based on artificial intelligence applications, blockchain and big data, digital communications, fintech and shipping services (Li, 2021). Together with anti-virus measures, economy maintenance and development policies are given by the government, public bodies, businesses, education centers, religious sites, families and individuals, therefore, work-from-home services are made as home deliveries, sales chat, takeaway food and beverages, home entertainment and online praying... More than 80% businesses know that their most beneficial work, operation process and marketing communications should be digitalized to remain survival and profitable in the hardest time of pandemic.

Changes in digital communications in COVID19 era

COVID-19 still impacts ts Vietnam's marketing communications and the country is currently in the 4th wave of outbreak. Digital communications in Vietnam are used not only for promoting brands and sales, but also for research projects for businesses to have better decision for their strategies. They have moved from web-based communications to more digital platforms as fan page, group page, chat applications and video contents. Digital content in many forms, including digital posters, digital videos, short clips, short advertorials are inserted and used in many platforms, especially Facebook, Zalo and Tiktok where the salespeople can chat directly with the consumers to give further information about the brands products. Communicators are expected to build online brand trust, brand love and brand loyalty when customers do not have chance to come in person to stores, showrooms or shopping malls, so, digital key messages are properly designed and conveyed to digital users. Digital transformation is not only applied to marketing communications, but also other business processes as sales, human resources, accounting and finance, production and logistics... in technology 4.0 era, but in COVID-19 time everything goes sharply digital (Nguyen, 2020).

Conclusion

Changes in digital communications are essential in coronavirus outbreak in four waves in Vietnam, especially to transforming digitally business entities in all of their business operations. This can be a good time for Vietnam's economy to go digital more rapidly in some models from digital services to sharing economy via diversified digital platforms. Limited in the four waves of SARS-CoV in Vietnam, the research is expected to analyze more statistical data, especially post-pandemic to have more obvious portrait of digital transformation in Vietnam's economy in general and in marketing communications particularly. Vietnam's initial success in covering the situation is a good encouragement to the country itself and other countries in a new normal life when the people have been accustomed to digital economy and digital entrepreneurship. This is also a punctual strategy for businesses to minimize losses in pandemic situations and follow this trend in a new normal situation for restructuring their operations in the coming years.

References and bibliography

1. AsiaPac. (2020). Vietnam Digital Marketing 2020. Retrieved: 8 June 2021, from: https://www.asiapacdigital.com/digital-marketing-insight/ vietnam-digital-marketing-2020
2. Cuong, P. H. (2019). Role of Digital Marketing in Consumer Goods Retailing. Evidence from Vietnam in the Context of the 4th Industrial Revolution. Journal of Advanced Research in Law and Economics (JARLE), 10(42), 1266-1273.
3. Doan, T. (2020). Developing a digital marketing plan for a small shop in Vietnam: May Bin-a cosmetics shop in Ho Chi Minh City.
4. Do, B. N., Tran, T. V., Phan, D. T., Nguyen, H. C., Nguyen, T. T., Nguyen, H. C., ... & Van Duong, T. (2020). Health Literacy, eHealth Literacy, Adherence to Infection Prevention and Control Procedures, Lifestyle Changes, and Suspected COVID-19 Symptoms Among Health Care Workers During Lockdown: Online Survey. Journal of medical Internet research, 22(11), e22894.

5. Hoang, T. D. L., Nguyen, H. K., & Nguyen, H. T. (2021). Towards an

economic recovery after the COVID-19 pandemic: empirical study on electronic commerce adoption of small and medium enterprises in Vietnam. Management & Marketing, 16(1).

6. Le, N., & Ratten, V. (2021). Digital Marketing and Social Entrepreneurship in Vietnam. In Developing Digital Marketing. Emerald Publishing Limited.
7. Li, S. (2021). How Does COVID-19 Speed the Digital Transformation of Business Processes and Customer Experiences? Review of business 41.1 (2021): 1–14. Print.
8. Nguyen, H., Nguyen, H. V., Le, N. B., Pham, T. T. T., & Nguyen, N. (2021). Online Book Fairs during the COVID-19 Pandemic: The experience of Vietnam. Logos, 32(1), 37-43.
9. Nguyen, T.H., Nguyen, V.Q., & Nguyen, T.T.M. (2021). Digital Transformation: Opportunities and Challenges for Leaders in the Emerging Countries in Response to Covid-19 Pandemic. Emerging Science Journal, 5, 21-36.
10. Nguyen, T. V. H. (2020). The Development of the Digital Economy in Vietnam. VNU Journal of Science: Economics and Business, 36(5E).
11. Statista. (2021). Actions taken when encountering online video advertisements among respondents in Vietnam in 2019. Retrieved: 7 June 2021, from: https://www.statista.com/statistics/1103261/vietnam-reactions-toward-online-video-ads/
12. Tien, N. H., Ngoc, N. M., Anh, D. B. H., Huong, N. D., Huong, N. T. T., & Phuong, T. N. M. (2020). Development opportunities for digital marketing in post Covid-19 period in Vietnam. Development, 1(5).
13. Tien, N. H., Ngoc, N. M., Anh, D. B. H., Huong, N. D., Huong, N. T. T., & Phuong, T. N. M. (2021). Challenges for service marketing in post Covid-19 period in Vietnam. International Journal of Multidisciplinary Research and Growth Evaluation. Volume 2; Issue 1; January-February 2021; Page No. 39-45.
14. Timvest. (2021). December 2020 Macroeconomic & Stock Market Highlights for Vietnam. Retrieved: 6 May 2021, from https://timvest.ch/december-2020-macroeconomic-stock-market-highlights-for-vietnam/
15. Tran, B. X., Nguyen, H. T., Le, H. T., Latkin, C. A., Pham, H. Q., Vu, L.

G., ... & Ho, R. C. (2020). Impact of COVID-19 on economic well-being and quality of life of the Vietnamese during the national social distancing. Frontiers in psychology, 11.

16. Trevisan, M., Le, L.C., Le, A.V. (2020). The COVID-19 Pandemic: A View from Vietnam. American journal of public health (1971) 110.8 (2020): 1152–1153. Web.

17. Vietnam Times. (2020). Hanoi launches "SmartCity" mobile app to track Covid-19 quarantined cases. Retrieved 27 April, from https://vietnamtimes.org.vn/hanoi-launches-smartcity-mobile-app-to-track-covid-19-quarantined-cases-18556.html.

Contact information

Name of the author: Liem, Bui Quoc (Bui, Q.L.)

Affiliation (University): Professional Communication Department, RMIT University, Ho Chi Minh City, Vietnam

Email: liem.buiquoc@rmit.edu.vn

Comparative Analysis of Integrated Marketing Communications Curriculum mid and postCovid 19: An "Eastmeets West" Examination of Integrated Marketing Communications Revision and Development Efforts

Jason Lee Carter

Abstract

Integrated Marketing Communications (IMC) is a business education degree focus receiving growing attention due to the advancement in communications technology, resources for global operations, and global corporations marketing strategies, and which has now increased substantially in the mid- and post-Covid 19 learning environment. The study targeted the challenges to IMC curriculum development to identify greater efficient curricula models tertiary institutions can use to modify their curriculum to meet these changing demands for the goal of achieving greater customer retention (student enrollment) and improved branding of the institution. A Grounded Theory (GT) approach analyzed IMC curricula from top rated western IMC programs to compare with eastern IMC programs. Findings showed homogeneous designs in western IMC curricula that prepared graduates for career success and subsequent higher retention rates, whereas eastern IMC programs customized for local career paths and lower retention. The conclusions infer standardization is key for an IMC degree program intended to prepare graduates for international careers, but customization is needed to prepare graduates for domestic careers. Recommendations are tertiary revision efforts should focus on determining the intention of the customer (student) career goals and adapt the IMC program accordingly.

Keywords: adult learner theory; curriculum development; curriculum standardization; grounded theory; integrated marketing communication

JEL Classification: A22, D83, M00

Introduction

The study examines the curriculum content of marketing communications' degree programs in eastern nations in order to identify the key curricula variations for success with counterpart programs in western cultures. The thesis is predicated on an analysis of Integrated Marketing Communications (IMC) degrees from successful western tertiary institutions, identifying the core elements of what makes them a successful IMC program, which retains customers and enhances the institution's branding strategies, and then identifying and comparing those western successes with the differing curriculum designs and implementation with eastern institutions and their subsequent outcomes. IMC is best defined as an approach to strategic planning for communicating brand aspects to target audiences requiring a coordination of the brand's marketing initiatives (Albinsson, Burman, Shows, & Stoddard, 2020). The aim of this study is to determine what differences in IMC curriculum results in greater success rates with outcomes being greater employability of program graduates, in order to target the deficiencies in eastern IMC programs in post-graduate, Master of Business Administration (MBA) degrees. Ultimately, such analysis therefore determines student enrollment growth rates and higher recognition of the institution's quality as a brand. Once identified, the results subsequently establish recommendations to tertiary institutions in their efforts for improving marketing curriculum revision and development, specifically for IMC programs, to be utilized in accomplishing that ultimate goal of greater retention and enhanced branding as the value proposition of the institution as a quality establishment capable of producing greater successful graduates.

As the concepts of global business transactions, specifically in marketing, increase, inherent with this need during increasingly difficult times for tertiary learning from Covid 19 impacts (Cao et al., 2020; Nicola, et al., 2020; Sahu, 2020), comes a demand to understand if there is an ideal

IMC program advisable for eastern tertiary institutions to utilize in those efforts that can be adapted from successful western marketing programs that have proven success and ratings, as discussed later in this study (Albinsson, Burman, Shows, & Stoddard, 2020). The various institutions around Asia utilize differing curricula outlines and guidelines in the design, implementation, and assessment of their IMC programs even before Covid 19 that do not meet international standards (Batra, & Keller, 2016; Camilleri, 2019; Melles, 2019), and consequently reduce the employability potential of the graduate seeking a career abroad (Abrizah, Noorhidawati, & Kiran, 2017; Carpenter, & Agrawal, 2018; Delcoure, Sale, & Scalan, 2016). The IMC programs existing in their respective tertiary institutions are classified into differing faculties such as business faculties, communications faculties, journalism faculties, etc., without any sense of commonality in purpose or consistency in curriculum that matches international standards (Carillo, 2017; Hashim, Mohd Yasin, & Ya'kob, 2020; Hizi, 2019). That fact is now highlighted for deficiency more so now than ever before because of the global pandemic caused by Covid 19 (Cao et al., 2020; Nicola, et al., 2020; Sahu, 2020). The rationale of this study is that the western IMC top rated programs follow a similar process in curriculum design that is both effective and consistent internationally, and that the highest rated eastern IMC programs continued lack of similar western success is due to the inconsistency in IMC curriculum design and implementation that limits their graduates' career potential and institutional branding.

Problem Statement

Asian nations contemporarily have a focus on enhancing their nation's global competitiveness whilst tackling shifts in performance expectations amongst competition using ever-increasing technology usage, but more so during the Covid 19 pandemic that demands cost-cutting and an emerging digital communications platform utilization never before seen in the world. China's Belt and Road Initiative (BRI), for example, is Beijing's growth and development strategy for the nation's economy by establishing trade and political ties to over seventy nations around the globe, and serves as the country's motivating drive in every sector of the economy including education (Belt and Road Forum, 2019; WorldBank.org/

BRI., 2018). Likewise, Thailand's commitment to social and economic development, specifically in improving poverty reduction through increased opportunities, is also inclusive of improving education that can be seen as contributory to their economic development strategy similar to China's BRI further depending on enhancing communication while cutting costs (OECD.org/Thailand, 2018). The issue prompting this study is the quality of those efforts, specifically for the desire to improve education not from the educational quality aspect alone, but for the impact such improvements have on the value proposition the institution represents to the student for the capability of producing graduates with skills and abilities that do not meet with international standards amid issues of increasing digitalization of the education environment from both competition and pandemic effects (Abrizah et al., 2017; Briggs et al., 2018; Cao et al., 2020; Macionis et al., 2019; Nicola et al., 2020; Sahu, 2020Wan et al., 2017). The overall issue is to focus on the quality of the IMC program in the face of increasing competitiveness, technology, and digitalization of said programs from Covid 19 responses that ultimately improves consumer utility and the end result of brand maximization, filling-in that deficiency gap in empirical research providing Asian tertiary institutions with sufficient data-driven guidelines on enhancing their marketing curricula, improving IMC programs and the subsequent value improvement to the institutional brand.

Literature Review

Covid 19 Impact on Tertiary Education

Before focus on IMC programs can be made, the impact of the Covid 19 pandemic on tertiary education in general affecting all programs in higher education must be addressed. The key issues facing tertiary education institutions focus first on the changed learning environment due to online learning necessities, in which the learning environment has changed forever (Cao et al., 2020; Nicola et al., 2020; Sahu, 2020). Cost-cutting initiatives, low student attendance/enrollment, greater tuition price scrutiny from parents and scholarship organizations due to the decreased economies personally and institutionally are all contributing to an evolving learning environment most scholars are not prepared for (Assunção Flores, & Gago, 2020; Bao, 2020; Crawford et al., 2020; Ferrell, & Ferrell, 2020; Sahu, 2020), and for which most tertiary institutions are striving to adapt to (Bao, 2020; Cao et al., 2020; Nicola et al., 2020; Peters et al., 2020; Thatcher et al., 2020; Toquero, 2020). Online education in whole or in part will become increasingly demanded (Ferrell, & Ferrell, 2020; Peters et al., 2020; Thatcher et al., 2020; Toquero, 2020), and then the goals and initiatives of enhancing the technology and methodologies of providing a competitive digital learning medium become the inherent issue for concern (Ferrell, & Ferrell, 2020; Graham, Achenreiner, McDermott, & Crosby, 2020; Kulkarni, & Vinuales, 2020), especially considering the high number of scholars and institutions reporting their difficulty with such changing demands (Assunção Flores, & Gago, 2020; Bao, 2020; Crawford et al., 2020; Ferrell, & Ferrell, 2020; Nicola et al., 2020; Peters et al., 2020; Sahu, 2020; Thatcher et al., 2020; Toquero, 2020). The role of IMC program developments, like any other subject of higher education, will also require adaptation to technological usage that carries inherent necessities for change in the program design and implementation (Albinsson et al., 2020; Laverie et al., 2020; Marcham et al., 2020). Whether or not the institution modifies its IMC programs based solely on goals of improving consumer utility (customer satisfaction) inherently improving institutional branding, or to also be inclusive of the demands from online and digital learning affecting the program design for standardization or customization is the enquiry affecting this study's thesis.

IMC's Role in Business Education

Estaswara (2016) states that Integrated Marketing Communications (IMC) is a continuing development of the marketing discipline, and thereby draws for a need for further research studies into educational programs. Tertiary institutions' motivation to update and improve their marketing communications' learning programs is assessed by the delivery of qualified graduates, so the need for comprehending the changing nature of the IMC focus is the inherent goal tertiary institutions should higher prioritize in said efforts (Albinsson, Burman, Shows, & Stoddard, 2020; Batra & Keller, 2016; Estaswara, 2016; Keller, 2016; Patti et al.,

2017). The online Marketing Dictionary from Monash University states the IMC is, "a strategic process used to plan, develop, execute and evaluate coordinated, measurable, persuasive brand communication programs to targeted relevant external and internal audiences in order to build long term brand value" (Monash/Mrktg.Dic., 2020). Curriculum revision and development efforts from a traditional approach are not sufficient in this regard (Batra & Keller, 2016; Camilleri, 2019; Patti et al., 2017; Royo-Vela & Hünermund, 2016; Saenko et al., 2016; Valos et al., 2017).

The importance of what IMC programs mean to tertiary education is the desire for increased international competitiveness, such as China's BRI. The dominance of western tertiary institutions' marketing communications' graduates that obtain greater career success (Creedon & Al-Khaja, 2019; Hashim et al., 2020; Melewar et al., 2018; Rutter et al., 2017) is the focus issue since eastern nations desire the same results (Baumann & Winzar, 2016; Hizi, 2019; Indarti et al., 2016; Sharma & Singh, 2018; Thyroff & Kilbourne, 2017). When viewing these outcomes amid the pandemic effects on tertiary education in general, the demands of technology and adaptation for IMC programs is complex than mere curriculum improvements considering the impact on the institutional value proposition (Albinsson et al., 2020; Laverie et al., 2020; Marcham et al., 2020).

Top IMC Western Programs

Copenhagen Business School

Denmark's Copenhagen Business School's MSc in Brand and Communications Management degree program is the top Palmes award winner with a full 5 Palmes award (eduniversal-ranking.com/CBS, 2020). The program focuses on the communications aspect to marketing integration roles. The degree is aimed at enhancing graduates' knowledge base and experiential learning for the specific promotion of an organization's branding efforts for strategic growth (CBS/MSc.Brand.Comm., 2019).

Northwestern University – Medill School of Journalism, Media, Integrated Marketing Communications

The United States' Northwestern University - Medill School of Journalism,

Media, and Integrated Marketing Communications' MSc Integrated Marketing Communications degree program is a 5 Palmes awardee (eduniversal-ranking.com/Northwestern, 2020) that focuses on communications integrating forms of media as it relates to political, economic, regulatory, mediation, and audience response mechanisms (Northwestern/MS.IMC, 2020). The degree aims to instil diversity in theoretical media and communications applications, conceptualized engagement practice from media and communications perspective, and empirical research opportunities on marketing communications in social influencing roles.

Bologna Business School – University of Bologna

Italy's Bologna Business School – University of Bologna's MSc in Marketing, Communication & New Media degree is a 4 Palmes program (eduniversal-ranking.com/Bologna, 2020) that focuses on the fundamentals of corporate communications from a marketing perspective that specifically deals with the organization-wide integration efforts to maximize efficiency and cost of the entire business's marketing schemes (Bologna/Business.School, 2020). While being an Italian institution, the program is conducted in English.

West Virginia University – Reed College of Media

The United States' West Virginia University – Reed College of Media's MSc in Integrated Marketing Communications degree is a 3 Palmes program (eduniversal-ranking.com/WVU, 2020) that teaches the fundamentals of integrating communications from marketing initiatives that targets the most effective manner of getting a strategic marketing message across to consumers that deals from consistency, persuasion, and reinforcement of the brand (WVU/What.Is.IMC?, 2020). Primary focuses deal with all aspects of integrating marketing strategies from a communications standpoint through advertising, public relations, direct marketing, social media, and sales and promotions.

Top IMC Eastern Programs

National Sun YatSen University

Taiwan's National Sun Yat-Sen University's MBA in Marketing

Communications degree is a 3 Palmes rated program, and the highest ranked institution among the ranking eastern nations by the Palmes award system (eduniversal-ranking.com/NSY-S.University, 2020). The first issue to be noticed is that, while the degree program is ranked the highest among Asian nations with IMC-related programs, the program is in-fact an MBA degree with special electives in IMC-focused curricula and not a specific IMC degree (NSY-S.University/MBA, 2020). Nevertheless, the specialized electives does constitute a comparable degree program with an IMC focus.

De La Salle University

The Philippines' De La Salle University's Master of Marketing Communications degree is a 3 Palmes rated program, and the second highest ranked institution in Asia (eduniversal-ranking.com/De.La.Salle, 2020). As seen with the National Sun Yat-Sen University, this program is also different from western programs in that it is only a master's degree; no master in arts or sciences (De.La.Salle/MaMC., 2020). The program is different than the National Sun Yat-Sen University's program in that the degree is specifically designed for marketing communications.

Chiang Mai University

Thailand's Chiang Mai University's M.A. Program in Integrated Communication degree is a 2 Palmes rated program (eduniversal-ranking.com/CMU, 2020), and while it is not the third highest ranked eastern university in terms of marketing communications degree programs, it is the third closest ranked program for IMC considerations. The program is generated specifically for marketing communications in a Master of Arts degree composition, and indirectly focuses on the components of marketing and communications integration (CMU/MaMC, 2019).

La Trobe University

To round-out the final consideration for eastern institutions, the inclusion of an Australian university might seem at first to be misaligned, but considering the proportionately large percentage of Australian students are from many Asian nations (Arkoudis, Dollinger, Baik, & Patience, 2019; French, & James, 2016; Tran, & Vu, 2018), and since Australia is closer to

Asian countries than it is to western nations, including La Trobe University is an appropriate measure for comparative analysis. Also, there are no other institutions in eastern, Asian nations rated on the Palmes system, so the next appropriate program is needed for a correlative analysis. Australia's La Trobe University's Master of Digital Marketing Communications degree is a 3 Palmes winner for the Oceania region (eduniversal-ranking.com/La.Trobe, 2020). The degree program focuses on the normal marketing communications courses and aims, but from an integration effort they call interdisciplinary marketing communications for marketing campaign designs that is more appropriate for an IMC program rather than only a digital marketing communications degree (LaTrobe/MDMC, 2020).

Standardized or Unique Curriculum Design

According to Cohen (2007), the results-based perspective should be the key consideration if a business curriculum revision and development effort were targeting a big business approach, but if targeting a local business aptitude, then cultural imperatives need to be the primary concern in revision and development efforts. The implication is that a separation in business curriculum objectives needs to be a primary design contributor that differentiates between the global corporate marketplace and the small-to- medium (SME) market. As this study is concerned with regional competitiveness improvement through the business curricula, namely the IMC programs amid pandemic effects, the local marketplace considerations can be ruled out.

Many studies have been conducted indicating the need for standardizing a business curriculum for ensuring the learner is prepared for a career with global operations in mind (Carillo, 2017; Carpenter & Agrawal, 2018; Djan & George, 2016; Kaplan, 2018; Kerkhoff, 2017; Nolan & Kurthakoti, 2017; Oluwatoyin, 2018; Ritter et al., 2018; Rollier, 2020; Schworm et al., 2017; Verger et al., 2017; Zhang et al., 2016). The opposing studies to a standardized curriculum to business education remark on the perceived loss of creativity derived from diversity

(Oladunjoye, 2018; Rushek, 2017; Sahlberg, 2016; Sharma et al., 2017; Sleeter & Carmona, 2017; Zhao & Gearin, 2016).

The Palmes system shows the standardized approach generates better qualified graduates for internationalized career paths, thereby warranting the higher Palmes ranking that is based largely on alumni success rates and international employers' recommendations (eduniversal-ranking.com/Palmes, 2020). The overall judgment in the argument for standardization in business curriculum, including marketing and communications program, versus customized and unique curricula more inclusive of local cultural aspects, comes down to the extensive study conducted by the United Nations Economic Commission for Europe (UNECE) in 2018. The study was conducted from 2012 to 2018 with the purpose of determining whether or not curriculum revision and development efforts at virtually every level of learners' university education experience should be standardization as per international considerations, or customized based on local cultural and heritage considerations (UNECE, 2018). The UNECE focused on the perspective of the working environment and career potential, where standards in areas involving the economics' focused course on international trade require a heavily-reliant learning objective(s) stemmed in global trade-and-commerce based on economic conditions and policies, as well as the implications of quality standards and the identification of sustainable production and consumption goals (UNECE, 2018, p.6); the implication being that any corporate entity conducting their operations across borders will need to have employees knowledgeable in "understanding of standards and standards-related issues" (p.6).

AACSB accredited, but only two of the four eastern IMC programs (i.e. National Sun Yat-sen University and La Trobe University) are accredited (AACSB/Accredited.Schools, 2020). There are several other recognized accrediting bodies with near or less-than reputations as the AACSB, such as the Accreditation Council for Collegiate Business Schools and Programs (ACBSP), the Council for Higher Education Accreditation (CHEA), the International Assembly for Collegiate Business Education (IACBE), the Association of MBAs (AMBA), and European Quality Improvement System (EQIS) (Zhao & Ferran, 2016). The overall message is that accreditation for a business program is the ultimate aim of the tertiary institution if it wants to remain, or even obtain, worldwide competitiveness.

Methodology & Research Questions

A grounded theory (GT) approach is utilized for the collected data of published degree curricula that outlines the programs of study for a comparative analysis of the western and eastern top-rated IMC degrees as the sample (n) statistic for the population (N) body of IMC degree programs. The programs selected for this study are based on their rankings in the Eduniversal organization that evaluates tertiary institutional programs' quality and efficiency across the globe (eduniversal- ranking.com/Eduniversal, 2020). Eduniversal's evaluation system for "Best 1,000 Business Schools in 154 countries ranking" (eduniversal- ranking.com/Ranking, 2020) targets the highest ranking business programs in what is termed the "Palmes of Excellence" (eduniversal- ranking.com/Palmes, 2020) award symbolized by a palm tree leaf, with the more 'Palmes' received the higher the ranking. Only those tertiary institutions with IMC programs receiving the highest Palmes award in relation to marketing communications and IMC degree programs are reviewed for this analysis. The collected information is then codified of the various programs observed, with indicator (dummy) variable designations offered by the Thematic software that is "a form of qualitative data analysis (QDA) that extracts themes from text by analyzing the word and sentence structure" (Thematic.Software, 2019), and helps to ensure bias avoidance.

A multiple linear regression (MLR) test for independence is used to determine if either regions' institutions show a consistency or inconsistency in program designs. The null determination is that a consistent program without change to international standards is the basis for the higher ratings. The alternative determination is that there is no consistency in the program designs that ultimately contributes to a degree not adherent to international expectancies. The highest rated tertiary institution in each region will be assumed as the dependent variable since it represents the benchmark that the other institutions aim to achieve, which are assigned as the independent variables for analysis, and is applied to both MLRs.

The second phase of the GT analysis is a test of reliability that confirms the variance in null-vs.-alternative outcomes from the MLR test for independence. For this purpose, a chi-square (X2) test for homogeneity confirms or rejects the reliability of comparative results between MLR tests. This is done in order to validate whether there is a true variation between the regional outcomes, or if there is no difference and invalidate the hypothesis that Palmes-ranked programs do not need a consistent design for effective fulfillment of employer and economy demands.

The research questions and associated hypotheses are thusly:

Research Question 1: Is there a consistency in western IMC degree programs that validate a higher Palmes ranking as adherent to international expectations of quality IMC graduates for personal career, local economy, and tertiary institutions' value proposition?

H10: There is no variation between western tertiary institutions' IMC program designs that in-turn contribute to higher Palmes ranking and international expectations of quality IMC graduates for personal career, local economy, and tertiary institution's growth and profit.

H1a: There is a variation between western tertiary institutions' IMC program designs that in-turn do not contribute to higher Palmes ranking and international expectations of quality IMC graduates for personal career, local economy, and tertiary institution's growth and profit.

Research Question 2: Is there a consistency in eastern IMC degree programs that validate a higher Palmes ranking as adherent to international expectations of quality IMC graduates for personal career, local economy, and tertiary institutions' value proposition?

H20: There is no variation between eastern tertiary institutions' IMC program designs that in-turn contribute to higher Palmes ranking and international expectations of quality IMC graduates for personal career, local economy, and tertiary institution's growth and profit.

H2a: There is a variation between eastern tertiary institutions' IMC program designs that in-turn do not contribute to higher Palmes ranking and international expectations of quality IMC graduates for personal career, local economy, and tertiary institution's growth and profit.

Research Question 3: If the H10 and the H2a are accepted, is there a plausible causality that is evident that explains the outcomes of the theorized homogenous IMC programs higher ranking and international acceptability that demonstrates why the heterogeneous IMC program designs do not achieve such recognition? As this will be a strictly qualitative final assessment, there will be no null or alternative hypotheses applicable.

Findings & Discussion

Research Question 1 MLR Outcomes

The MLR test results for the western tertiary institutions' IMC programs showed the predictable consistency the study's thesis. The R2 comes out at a perfect whole 1, and the Adj.-R2 outcome is 0.8, and relatively close enough to whole 1 to indicate there is quite literally very little difference in curriculum design. The implications confirm the H10 that there is no deviation in curriculum amongst the top-ranked IMC program in western tertiary institutions and rejecting the H1a. The subsequent inference therefore is an acknowledgement of the higher ranking and career success of graduates in MBA degrees concentrating in IMC programs that adheres to a standardization of curricula universally acceptable across the world. As all four of the western institutions' IMC programs are higher ranked than the eastern institutions' IMC programs, this standardization becomes a recommendation for eastern institutions' focus for revision that standardizes their curricula to meet those international standards.

Research Question 2 MLR Outcomes

The MLR test results for the eastern tertiary institutions' IMC programs showed an inconsistency in design that the study's thesis predicted. The R2 comes out at 0.471663749 that is far enough from 1 to constitute a judgment of non-linearity, but it is with the Adj.-R2 outcome of 0.075411561 that the deviation is more obvious that there is very little similarity in curriculum design among eastern tertiary institutions. The implications confirm the H2a that there is a significant difference in curriculum amongst the top-ranked IMC program in eastern tertiary institutions, with the H20 therefore being rejected. Again, the inference when comparing the rankings of the western versus eastern IMC programs validates the recommendation for eastern programs to standardize their curricula if the intention is to gain those higher international rankings as the western IMC programs have achieved. The individualized and inconsistent programs do not validate graduates' career potential since the degrees conferred do not hold to international expectancies.

Research Question 3 Outcome

RQ3 is the final comparison of the n of four western institutions against four eastern institutions. The outcomes indicate that all four IMC programs in western programs show a standardization and consistency in learning objectives since they are all four designated as Master of Science (MSc) degrees: i.e. the Copenhagen Business School: MSc in Brand and Communications Management; the Northwestern University - Medill School of Journalism, Media, and Integrated Marketing Communications: MSc Integrated Marketing Communications; the Bologna Business School – University of Bologna: MSc in Marketing, Communication & New Media; and the West Virginia University – Reed College of Media: MSc in Integrated Marketing Communications. This is a common trait that considers an IMC degree as a science focus within a business faculty paradigm that concentrates on the universally relevant subjects based in the sciences, such as mathematical analytics, statistics, diplomatic communication, finance, economics, etc. (Kaur, 2019; Keller, 2018; Melles, 2019; Pook et al., 2017; Stevens et al., 2019).

The counter to this approach is seen in the eastern IMC programs that are identified as an arts-related degree that focuses more on history, language, religion, etc. to round-out the business educational experience (Hummel et al., 2018; Ingold, 2018; Nahornick, 2016; Robertson, 2018), and is appropriate for degrees based on a domestic context rather than internationalization: i.e. the National Sun Yat-Sen University: MBA in Marketing Communications; the De La Salle University: Master of Marketing Communications; the Chiang Mai University: M.A. Program in Integrated Communication; and the La Trobe University: Master of Digital Marketing Communications.

As per the AACSB guidelines, an effective assessment of the student's knowledge and skillset is a final evaluation of a cognitive nature. For western IMC programs, all four of the n IMC institutions' final assessment is a marketing project involving research, design, proposal, and application of a project that cultivates the knowledge incurred throughout the degree program's core courses. For the n eastern IMC programs, only Thailand's Chiang Mai University's M.A. Program in Integrated Communication has a similar final assessment. Neither the National Sun Yat-Sen University: MBA in Marketing Communications, the De La Salle University: Master of Marketing Communications, nor the La Trobe University: Master of Digital Marketing Communications has any assessment.

Conclusions and Recommendations

The key consideration of revising and developing a curriculum with an IMC focus amid a global pandemic and increasing competitiveness is the determination between international or domestic ambitions. If the program is to be domestically-focused then the curriculum should be customized and not follow any international standard if that is deemed to be the intention, but one that does not seem relevant to the development goals with increased international competitiveness. Further, the inherent consequence is that the programs' designs do not consider graduates' career potential outside of their home region or neighboring eastern Asian nations. The overall impact on the institution's branding as a value proposition will attract consumers (students) based on their own career goals of obtaining a career with global businesses or a career domestically, and serve as the institution's guiding motivation in their specific IMC revision and development goals based on the type of student they want to attract and retain.

The western IMC programs adhere to an international set of standards, with all four of the sampled western IMC programs designated as MSc degree programs design that encompasses more scientific-based courses like mathematical analytics, statistics, diplomatic communication, finance, economics, etc. acceptable from a universally desired set of knowledge and skillsets. The UNECE and accreditation agencies call for a standardized curricula across the world is a demand for the skills and abilities of a graduate prepared to operate in consideration of varying marketplaces regardless of cultural inclinations. The skillsets need to be adaptable to any market using the common communication techniques akin to mathematical analytics, statistics, diplomatic communication, finance, economics, etc. While the UNECE and accreditation agencies policies and guidelines were formatted well-before the Covid 19 outbreak, their expectancies have become even more relevant today in guiding tertiary institution efforts in seeing the benefit to improving their IMC curriculum, the standards' improvement from such efforts, the consumer utility improvements from those efforts, and the ending value proposition enhancement as the final outcome of said efforts.

Future research should focus on similar cross-cultural examinations of tertiary programs for efficiency in producing graduates with enhance employability potential for global operations especially involving an integrated marketing communications. The focus should be targeting the business education subjects that focus on conducting market research, market analysis, market design, global distribution, consumer identification, global competition strategizing, and project-based experience from a perspective of a science-related program or faculty.

References

1. AACSB/Mission. (2020). What We Do. Association to Advance Collegiate Schools of Business. https://www.aacsb.edu/about/mission

2. Abrizah, A., Noorhidawati, A., & Kiran, K. (2017). Global Visibility of Asian Universities' Open Access Institutional Repositories. Malaysian Journal of Library & Information Science, 15(3), 53-73. https://mjlis.um.edu.my/article/ view/6942

3. Albinsson, P. A., Burman, B., Shows, G. D., & Stoddard, J. E. (2020). Integrating and assessing student perceived sustainability literacy in an integrated marketing communications course. Marketing Education Review, 1-18. https://doi.org/10.1080/10528008.2020.1770102

4. Arkoudis, S., Dollinger, M., Baik, C., & Patience, A. (2019). International students' experience in Australian higher education: can we do better?. Higher Education, 77(5), 799-813. https://doi.org/10.1007/s10734-018-0302-x

5. Assunção Flores, M., & Gago, M. (2020). Teacher education in times of COVID-19 pandemic in Portugal: National, institutional and pedagogical

responses. Journal of Education for Teaching, 1-10. https://doi.org/10.1080/02607476.2020.1799709
6. Bao, W. (2020). COVID-19 and online teaching in higher education: A case study of Peking University. Human Behavior and Emerging Technologies, 2(2), 113-115. https://doi.org/10.1002/hbe2.191
7. Batra, R., & Keller, K. L. (2016). Integrating marketing communications: New findings, new lessons, and new ideas. Journal of Marketing, 80(6), 122- 145. https://doi.org/10.1509/jm.15.0419
8. Baumann, C., & Winzar, H. (2016). The role of secondary education in explaining competitiveness. Asia Pacific Journal of Education, 36(1), 13-30. https://doi.org/10.1080/02188791.2014.924387
9. Beard, D., Schweiger, D., & Surendran, K. (2019). Integrating soft skills assessment through university, college, and programmatic efforts at an AACSB accredited institution. Journal of Information Systems Education, 19(2), 11. https://aisel.aisnet.org/jise/vol19/iss2/11
10. Belt and Road Forum. (2019). Belt and Road Forum for International Cooperation. Belt and Road Forum. http://www.beltandroadforum2019.com/ conference-profile/overview/
11. Bologna/Business.School. (2020). Master in Marketing, Communication & New Media. Bologna Business School – University of Bologna. https://www.bbs.unibo.eu/master-fulltime/master-in-new-media- and-marketing-communication/
12. Bologna/Cntnt.Mrktg.Lab. (2020). Content Marketing Laboratory. Bologna Business School – University of Bologna. https://www.bbs.unibo.eu/master-fulltime/master-in-new-media-and-marketing-communication/#courses_2
13. Bologna/Comm./Story. (2020). Communications and Storytelling. Bologna Business School – University of Bologna. https://www.bbs.unibo.eu/master-fulltime/master-in-new-media-and-marketing-communication/#courses_1
14. Bologna/Corp.Comm. (2020). Corporate Communication. Bologna Business School – University of Bologna. https://www.bbs.unibo.eu/

master-fulltime/master-in-new-media-and-marketing-communication/#courses_3

15. Bologna/CRM/Mrktg.Rrsch. (2020). CRM and Marketing Research. Bologna Business School – University of Bologna. https://www.bbs.unibo.eu/master-fulltime/master-in-new-media-and-marketing-communication/#courses_4
16. Bologna/Dig.Int.Mrktg. (2020). Digital Interactive Marketing. Bologna Business School – University of Bologna. https://www.bbs.unibo.eu/master-fulltime/master-in-new-media-and-marketing-communication/#courses_6
17. Bologna/Mrktg. (2020). Marketing. Bologna Business School – University of Bologna. https://www.bbs.unibo.eu/master-fulltime/master-in-new-media-and-marketing-communication/#courses_10
18. Bologna/Sls.Trd.Mrktg. (2020). Sales and Trade Marketing. Bologna Business School – University of Bologna. https://www.bbs.unibo.eu/master-fulltime/master-in-new-media-and-marketing-communication/#courses_12
19. Bologna/Strtgc.Acct. (2020). Strategic Accounting. Bologna Business School – University of Bologna. https://www.bbs.unibo.eu/master-fulltime/master-in-new-media-and-marketing-communication/#courses_14
20. Briggs, J. G., Dearden, J., & Macaro, E. (2018). English medium instruction: Comparing teacher beliefs in secondary and tertiary education. Studies in Second Language Learning and Teaching, 8(3). https://doi.org/ 10.14746/ssllt.2018.8.3.7
21. Camilleri, M. A. (2019). Higher Education Marketing: Opportunities and Challenges in the Digital Era. Camilleri, MA (2019). Higher Education Marketing: Opportunities and Challenges in the Digital Era. Academia, 0(16-17), 4-28. https://doi.org/10.26220/aca.3169
22. Cao, W., Fang, Z., Hou, G., Han, M., Xu, X., Dong, J., & Zheng, J. (2020). The psychological impact of the COVID-19 epidemic on college students in China. Psychiatry Research, 112934. https://doi.org/10.1016/j.psychres.2020.112934

23. Carillo, K. D. A. (2017). Let's stop trying to be "sexy": Preparing managers for the (big) data-driven business era. Business Process Management Journal, 34(3), 60-77. https://doi.org/10.23925/2237-4418.2019v34i3p60-77

24. Carpenter, D. A., & Agrawal, V. K. (2018). Infusing information technology into the core business curriculum: a change management project. The Journal of Business Inquiry, 7(1), 3-20. https://journals.uvu.edu/index.php/jbi/article/view/161

25. CBS/KAN-CBCMO1000U. (2019). Perspectives on Consumer Behaviour. Copenhagen Business School. https://kursuskatalog.cbs.dk/2019-2020/KAN- CBCMO1000U.aspx

26. CBS/KAN-CBCMO1002U. (2019). Marketing Communication. Copenhagen Business School. https://kursuskatalog.cbs.dk/2019-2020/KAN-CBCMO1002U.aspx

27. CBS/KAN-CBCMO1008U. (2019). Marketing Accounting and Brand Performance. Copenhagen Business School. https://kursuskatalog.cbs.dk/2019-2020/KAN-CBCMO1008U.aspx

28. CBS/KAN-CBCMO1009U. (2019). Perspectives in Strategic Brand Management. Copenhagen Business School. https://kursuskatalog.cbs.dk/2019-2020/KAN-CBCMO1009U.aspx

29. CBS/KAN-CBCMO1010U. (2019). Applied Strategic Brand Management. Copenhagen Business School. https://kursuskatalog.cbs.dk/2019-2020/KAN- CBCMO1010U.aspx

30. CBS/KAN-CBCMO1011U. (2019). Scientific Marketing Project. Copenhagen Business School. https://kursuskatalog.cbs.dk/2019-2020/KAN-CBCMO1011U.aspx

31. CBS/KAN-CBCMO1020U. (2019). Neuroscience of Branding. Copenhagen Business School. https://kursuskatalog.cbs.dk/2019-2020/KAN-CBCMO1020U.aspx

32. CBS/KAN-CBCMO1801U. (2019). Social Media From A Branding Perspective. Copenhagen Business School. https://kursuskatalog.cbs.dk/2019-2020/KAN-CBCMO1801U.aspx

33. CBS/MSc.Brand.Comm. (2019). MSc in Economics and Business Administration - Brand and Communications Management. Copenhagen Business School.

https://www.cbs.dk/uddannelse/kandidat/candmerc/

marketing/msc-in-economics-and-business-administration-brand-and-communications-management
34. CMU/MC701. (2019). MC701 Paradigm and Communication Studies.

Chiang Mai University. https://mis.cmu.ac.th/TQF/coursepublic/851701.aspx
35. CMU/MC702. (2019). MC702 Principles and Theory of Integrated Communication. Chiang Mai University. https://mis.cmu.ac.th/TQF/coursepublic/851702.aspx
36. CMU/MC703. (2019). MC703 Professional Ethics and Law of Communication. Chiang Mai University. https://mis.cmu.ac.th/TQF/coursepublic/851703.aspx
37. CMU/MC705. (2019). MC705 Media and Society Seminar. Chiang Mai University. https://mis.cmu.ac.th/TQF/coursepublic/851705.aspx
38. CMU/MC706. (2019). MC706 Qualitative Communication Research. Chiang Mai University. https://mis.cmu.ac.th/TQF/coursepublic/851706.aspx
39. CMU/MC707. (2019). MC707 Quantitative Communication Research. Chiang Mai University. https://mis.cmu.ac.th/TQF/coursepublic/851707.aspx
40. CMU/MC754. (2019). MC754 Integrated Marketing Communication Process. Chiang Mai University. https://mis.cmu.ac.th/TQF/coursepublic/851754.aspx
41. CMU/MC798. (2019). MC798 Independent Study. Chiang Mai University. https://mis.cmu.ac.th/TQF/coursepublic/851798.aspx
42. CMU/MaMC. (2019). Chiang Mai University: M.A. Program in Integrated Communication. Chiang Mai University. https://www.cmu.ac.th/en/faculty/ mass_communication/aboutus
43. Cohen, E. (2007). Information and Beyond, Part 1: Issues in Informing Science and Information Technology, Volume 4. p.390. ISI Press.
44. Crawford, J., Butler-Henderson, K., Rudolph, J., Malkawi, B., Glowatz, M., Burton, R., ... & Lam, S. (2020). COVID-19: 20 countries' higher education intra-period digital pedagogy responses. Journal of Applied Learning & Teaching, 3(1), 1-20. http://dx.doi.org/10.37074/jalt.2020.3.1.7
45. Creedon, P., & Al-Khaja, M. (2019). An overview of Middle East public relations practice, education, and research from isolation to globalization. Journal of Public Relations Research, 31(3-4), 84-96. https://doi.org/10.1080/1062726X.2019.1682324

46. De.La.Salle/MaMC. (2020). De La Salle University: Master of Marketing Communications. https://www.dlsu.edu.ph/colleges/rvrcob/graduate-degree-programs/master-of-marketing-communications/

47. Delcoure, N., Sale, M. L., & Scalan, G. (2016). Institutionalizing and Standardizing Assessment Methodology for Multiple Accreditation Agencies. Business Education & Accreditation, 8(1), 1-14. https://papers.ssrn.com/sol3/papers.cfm?abstract_id=2825392

48. Djan, J., & George, B. (2016). Standardization or Localization: A Study of Online Learning Programmes by Tertiary Institutions in Ghana. European Journal of Contemporary Education, 18(4), 430-437. https://doi.org/ 10.13187/ejced.2016.18.430

49. Djoundourian, S. S. (2017). Assessment of learning in business education: Standardized or homegrown?. Journal of Education for Business, 92(5), 238-244. https://doi.org/10.1080/08832323.2017.1339662

50. eduniversal-ranking.com/Bologna. (2020). 4-Palmes award: Bologna Business School - University of Bologna: Master in Marketing, Communication & New Media. Eduniversal Group. https://www.best-masters.com/ranking-master-corporate-communication-in-western-europe/master-in-marketing-communication-new-media-bologna-business-school-university-of-bologna.html

51. eduniversal-ranking.com/CBS. (2020). 5-Palmes award: Copenhagen Business School: MSc in Brand and Communications Management / Marketing Communication Management. Eduniversal Group. https://www.best-masters.com/ranking-master-corporate-communication-in-western-europe/msc-in-brand-and-communications-management-marketing-communication-management-copenhagen-business-school.html

52. eduniversal-ranking.com/CMU. (2020). 2-Palmes award: Chiang Mai University: M.A. Program in Integrated Communication. Eduniversal Group. https://www.best-masters.com/ranking-master-corporate-communication-in-far-eastern-asia/m-a-in-communication-studies-chiang-mai-university.html

53. eduniversal-ranking.com/De.La.Salle. (2020). 3-Palmes award: De La Salle University: Master of Marketing Communications. Eduniversal Group.

https://www.best-masters.com/ranking-master-corporate-communication-
in-far-eastern-asia/master-of-marketing-communications-de-la-salle-university.html

54. eduniversal-ranking.com/La.Trobe. (2020). 3-Palmes award: La Trobe University: Master of Digital Marketing Communications. Eduniversal Group.

https://www.best-masters.com/ranking-master-e-business-and-digital-marketing-in-oceania/master-of-digital-marketing-communications-la-trobe-university.html
55. eduniversal-ranking.com/Northwestern. (2020). 5-Palmes award: Northwestern University - Medill School of Journalism, Media, and Integrated Marketing Communication: MSc Integrated Marketing Communications. Eduniversal Group. https://www.best-masters.com/ranking-master-e- business-and-digital-marketing-in-north-america/ms-integrated-marketing- communications-northwestern-university-medill-school-of-journalism-media- integrated-marketing-communications.html
56. eduniversal-ranking.com/NSY-S.University. (2020). 3-Palmes award: National Sun Yat-Sen University: MBA in Marketing Communications. Eduniversal Group. https://www.best-masters.com/ranking-master- corporate-communication-in-far-eastern-asia/mba-in-marketing- communications-national-sun-yat-sen-university.html
57. eduniversal-ranking.com/Ranking. (2020). Official Ranking of the Best 1000 Business Schools. Eduniversal Group. https://eduniversal-ranking.com/ methodology/official-selection-of-the-best-business-schools.html
58. eduniversal-ranking.com/Palmes. (2020). Eduniversal Rating: Palmes of Excellence. Eduniversal Group. https://eduniversal-ranking.com/ methodology/entering-the-system-or-obtaining-an-additional-palme-of-
59. eduniversal-ranking.com/WVU. (2020). 3-Palmes award: West Virginia University - Reed College of Media: Integrated Marketing Communications. Eduniversal Group. https://www.best-masters.com/ranking-master- corporate-communication-in-north-america/integrated-marketing- communications-west-virginia-university-reed-college-of-media.html
60. Estaswara, H. (2016). Integrated marketing communications (IMC) in higher education in Indonesia. Polish Journal of Management Studies 14(1), 74-83. https://www.researchgate.net/publication/

312050316_Integrated_marketing_communications_IMC_in_higher_educatio
n_in_Indonesia#:~:text=Purpose%20%E2%80%93%20The%20emergence
%20of%20integrated,development%20in%20the%20marketing%20disciplin
e.&text=Originality%2Fvalue%20%E2%80%93%20Indicates%20a%20need,
management%2C%20marketing%20and%20marketing%20communications

61. Ferrell, O. C., & Ferrell, L. (2020). Technology challenges and opportunities facing marketing education. Marketing Education Review, 30(1), 3-14. https://doi.org/10.1080/10528008.2020.1718510
62. French, S., & James, R. (2016). Australian higher education. In The Palgrave Handbook of Asia Pacific Higher Education. Palgrave Macmillan.
63. Graham, K. W., Achenreiner, G., McDermott, M., & Crosby, E. (2020). Is what students want what they really need? A values view of undergraduate marketing elective course offerings. Marketing Education Review, 1-10. https://doi.org/10.1080/10528008.2020.1773277
64. Hashim, S., Mohd Yasin, N., & Ya'kob, S. A. (2020). What constitutes student–university brand relationship? Malaysian students' perspective. Journal of Marketing for Higher Education, 1-23. https://doi.org/10.1080/08841241.2020.1713278
65. Hizi, G. (2019). Marketised "Educational Desire" and the Impetus for Self-improvement: The Shifting and Reproduced Meanings of Higher Education in Contemporary China. Asian Studies Review, 43(3), 493-511. https://doi.org/10.1080/10564934.2014.995532
66. Hummel, K., Pfaff, D., & Rost, K. (2018). Does economics and business education wash away moral judgment competence?. Journal of Business Ethics, 150(2), 559-577. https://doi.org/10.1007/s10551-016-3142-6
67. Indarti, N., Rostiani, R., & Nastiti, T. (2016). Underlying factors of entrepreneurial intentions among Asian students. The South East Asian Journal of Management, 1(1), 143-160. https://doi.org/10.21002/seam.v4i2.5636
68. Ingold, T. (2018). From science to art and back again: The pendulum of an anthropologist. Interdisciplinary Science Reviews, 43(3-4), 213-227. https://doi.org/10.1080/03080188.2018.1524234
69. Kaplan, A. (2018). A school is "a building that has four walls... with tomorrow inside": Toward the reinvention of the business school. Business Horizons, 61(4), 599-608. https://doi.org/10.1016/j.bushor.2018.03.010
70. Kaur, G. (2019). Is obsession with data and analytics making future marketers analytical researchers? A conceptual customer relationship

marketing model for customized marketing education. Journal of Education for Business, 94(8), 569-575. https://doi.org/10.1080/08832323.2019.1580245

71. Keller, G. F. (2018). Proposing Alternative Masters Degrees Models for Small Colleges/Schools of Business. Journal of Entrepreneurial Organization Management, 7, 232. DOI: 10.4172/2169-026X.1000232

72. Keller, K. L. (2016). Unlocking the power of integrated marketing communications: How integrated is your IMC program?. Journal of Advertising, 45(3), 286-301. https://doi.org/10.1080/00913367.2016.1204967

73. Kerkhoff, S. N. (2017). Designing global futures: A mixed methods study to develop and validate the teaching for global readiness scale. Teaching and Teacher Education, 65, 91-106. https://doi.org/10.1016/j.tate.2017.03.011

74. Kulkarni, G., & Vinuales, G. (2020). The importance of course title and student perceived value of a course to employers in motivating students to enroll in quantitative marketing courses. Marketing Education Review, 1-11. https://doi.org/10.1080/10528008.2020.1794900

75. LaTrobe/BUS5IAF. (2020). Introduction to Accounting and Finance. La Trobe University. https://www.latrobe.edu.au/students/your-course/subjects/ 2020/BUS5IAF

76. LaTrobe/BUS5POE. (2020). Principles of Economics. La Trobe University. https://www.latrobe.edu.au/students/your-course/subjects/2020/BUS5POE

77. LaTrobe/BUS5SBF. (2020). Statistics for Business and Finance. La Trobe University. https://www.latrobe.edu.au/students/your-course/subjects/2020/ BUS5SBF

78. LaTrobe/BUS5SMM2020. (2020). Sustainable Management & Marketing. La Trobe University. https://www.latrobe.edu.au/students/your-course/subjects/2020/BUS5SMM

79. LaTrobe/JRN5SMP. (2020). Social Media Practice and Journalism. La Trobe University. https://www.latrobe.edu.au/students/your-course/subjects/ 2020/JRN5SMP
80. LaTrobe/MDMC. (2020). La Trobe University: Master of Digital Marketing Communications. La Trobe University. eduhttps://www.latrobe.edu.au/ courses/master-of-digital-marketing-communications
81. LaTrobe/MKT5ACD. (2020). Advanced Consumer Decision Making. La

Trobe University. https://www.latrobe.edu.au/students/your-course/subjects/2020/MKT5ACD
82. LaTrobe/MKT5DMA. (2020). Digital Marketing. La Trobe University. https://www.latrobe.edu.au/students/your-course/subjects/2020/MKT5DMA
83. LaTrobe/MKT5MMA. (2020). Marketing Management. La Trobe University. https://www.latrobe.edu.au/students/your-course/subjects/2020/ MKT5MMA
84. Laverie, D., Humphrey, W., Manis, K. T., & Freberg, K. (2020). The digital era has changed marketing: a guide to using industry certifications and exploration of student perceptions of effectiveness. Marketing Education Review, 30(1), 57-80. https://doi.org/10.1080/10528008.2020.1716806
85. Macionis, N., Walters, G., & Kwok, E. (2019). International tertiary student experience in Australia: A Singaporean perspective. Journal of Hospitality, Leisure, Sport & Tourism Education, 25, 100174. https://doi.org/ 10.1016/j.jhlste.2018.10.002
86. Marcham, C. L., Ade, A. M., Clark, P., & Marion, J. (2020). Bias and trends in student evaluations in online higher education settings. The Collegiate Aviation Review International, 38(2). http://ojs.library.okstate.edu/ osu/index.php/cari
87. Melewar, T. C., Foroudi, P., Dinnie, K., & Nguyen, B. (2018). The role of corporate identity management in the higher education sector: an exploratory case study. Journal of Marketing Communications, 24(4), 337-359. https://doi.org/10.1080/13527266.2017.1414073
88. Melles, G. (2019). Views on education for sustainable development (ESD) among lecturers in UK MSc taught courses. International Journal of Sustainability in Higher Education. https://www.emerald.com/insight/content/ doi/10.1108/IJSHE-02-2018-0032/full/html
89. Mills, R. J., Velasquez, N. F., Fadel, K. J., & Bell, C. C. (2019). Examining IS curriculum profiles and the IS 2010 model curriculum

guidelines in AACSB-accredited schools. Journal of Information Systems Education, 23(4),
8. https://aisel.aisnet.org/jise/vol23/iss4/8

90. Monash/Mrktg.Dic. (2020). Integrated Marketing Communication (IMC). Monash University. https://www.monash.edu/business/marketing/marketing-dictionary/i/integrated-marketing-communication-imc

91. Nahornick, A. (2016). Math Matters: Comparison of the Mathematics Requirements for Bachelor of Arts and Bachelor of Science Degrees in Canada. Canadian Journal of Higher Education, 46(1), 109-120. https://files.eric.ed.gov/fulltext/EJ1098270.pdf

92. Nicola, M., Alsafi, Z., Sohrabi, C., Kerwan, A., Al-Jabir, A., Iosifidis, C., ... & Agha, R. (2020). The socio-economic implications of the coronavirus pandemic (COVID-19): A review. International Journal of Surgery (London, England), 78, 185. https://dx.doi.org/10.1016%2Fj.ijsu.2020.04.018

93. Nolan, M. A., & Kurthakoti, R. (2017). Experience matters: The differential impact of pedagogy on students' cultural intelligence–An exploratory study. Journal of Higher Education Theory and Practice, 17(3), 103-112. http://www.na-businesspress.com/JHETP/NolanMA_Web17_3_.pdf

94. Northwestern/Consumer.Insight. (2020). Consumer Insight. Northwestern University. https://www.medill.northwestern.edu/imc/full-time/curriculum/ consumer-insight.html

95. Northwestern/Fin.Acct. (2020). Financial Accounting. Northwestern University. https://www.medill.northwestern.edu/imc/full-time/curriculum/ financial-accounting.html

96. Northwestern/IMC.I. (2020). IMC I: Marketing Strategy. Northwestern University. https://www.medill.northwestern.edu/imc/full-time/curriculum/ imc-1-marketing-strategy.html

97. Northwestern/IMC.II. (2020). IMC II: Strategic Process. Northwestern University. https://www.medill.northwestern.edu/imc/full-time/curriculum/ imc-2-strategic-process.html

98. Northwestern/Immersion. (2020). Immersion Quarter. Northwestern University. https://www.medill.northwestern.edu/imc/full-time/exclusive- opportunities/immersion-quarter.html

99. Northwestern/Md.Fndtns. (2020). Media Foundations. Northwestern University. https://www.medill.northwestern.edu/imc/full-time/curriculum/ media-foundations.html

100. Northwestern/Mrkt.Rsrch. (2020). Marketing Research. Northwestern University. https://www.medill.northwestern.edu/imc/full-time/curriculum/ marketing-research.html
101. Northwestern/MS.IMC. (2020). Full-Time Master of Science in Integrated

Marketing Communications. Northwestern University. https://www.medill.northwestern.edu/imc/full-time/index.html
102. Northwestern/Stgc.Comm. (2020). Strategic Communications Foundations. Northwestern University. https://www.medill.northwestern.edu/ imc/full-time/curriculum/strategic-communications-foundations.html
103. NSY-S.University/MBA. (2020). Master of Business Administration Program in International Business (IBMBA). National Sun Yat-Sen University. https://www.ibmba-nsysu.com/course-list
104. OECD.org/Thailand. (2018). Thailand - OECD. Organization for Economic Cooperation and Development. https://www.oecd.org/dev/asia- pacific/saeo-2019-Thailand.pdf
105. Oladunjoye, T. G. (2018). Optimizing business education for national development. Nigerian Journal of Business Education (NIGJBED), 3(1), 1-16. http://www.nigjbed.com.ng/index.php/nigjbed/article/viewFile/3/3
106. Oluwatoyin, D. M. (2018). Business Education Teacher-An Instrument for Integrating New Business Education Technologies for Sustainable Development Practice. The Educational Review, USA, 2(6), 360-370. https:// doi.org/10.26855/er.2018.06.005
107. Patti, C. H., Hartley, S. W., van Dessel, M. M., & Baack, D. W. (2017). Improving integrated marketing communications practices: A comparison of objectives and results. Journal of Marketing Communications, 23(4), 351- 370. https://doi.org/10.1080/13527266.2015.1027251
108. Peters, M. A., Wang, H., Ogunniran, M. O., Huang, Y., Green, B., Chunga, J. O., ... & Khomera, S. W. (2020). China's internationalized higher education during Covid-19: Collective student autoethnography. Postdigital Science and Education, 1. https://doi.org/10.1007/s42438-020-00128-1
109. Phillips, M., Howard, H., Vaaler, A., & Hubbard, D. E. (2019). Mapping industry standards and integration opportunities in business management curricula. Journal of Business & Finance Librarianship, 24(1-2), 17-29. https://doi.org/10.1080/08963568.2019.1638662

110. Pook, A. S. Y., Chong, C. W., & Yuen, Y. Y. (2017). Effectiveness of cross-border knowledge transfer in Malaysian MSC status corporations. Knowledge Management & E-Learning: An International Journal, 9(1), 90-110. https://doi.org/10.34105/j.kmel.2017.09.006

111. Ritter, B. A., Small, E. E., Mortimer, J. W., & Doll, J. L. (2018). Designing management curriculum for workplace readiness: Developing students' soft skills. Journal of Management Education, 42(1), 80-103. https://doi.org/10.1177/1052562917703679

112. Robertson, R. (2018). Glocalization. The International Encyclopedia of Anthropology, 1-8. https://doi.org/10.1002/9781118924396.wbiea2275

113. Rollier, B. (2020). Preparing MIS students for a global economy. Journal of Information Systems Education, 12(4), 2. https://aisel.aisnet.org/jise/vol12/iss4/2

114. Royo-Vela, M., & Hünermund, U. (2016). Effects of inbound marketing communications on HEIs' brand equity: the mediating role of the student's decision-making process. An exploratory research. Journal of Marketing for Higher Education, 26(2), 143-167. https://doi.org/10.1080/08841241.2016.1233165

115. Rushek, K. A. (2017). The global education reform movement and its effect on the local African American community. Diaspora, Indigenous, and Minority Education, 11(3), 139-147. https://doi.org/10.1080/15595692.2016.1219848

116. Rutter, R., Lettice, F., & Nadeau, J. (2017). Brand personality in higher education: anthropomorphized university marketing communications. Journal of Marketing for Higher Education, 27(1), 19-39. https://doi.org/10.1080/08841241.2016.1213346

117. Saenko, N. R., Sozinova, A. A., Karabulatova, I. S., Akhmetov, I. V., Mamatelashvili, O. V., & Pismennaya, E. E. (2016). Research in action integrated marketing communications as the elements of information and virtualization market relations. International Review of Management and Marketing, 6(1), 267-272. https://doi.org/10.34069/AI/2020.29.05.38

118. Sahlberg, P. (2016). The global educational reform movement and its impact on schooling. The handbook of global education policy, 1(1), 128-144. https://doi.org/10.1002/9781118468005.ch7

119. Sahu, P. (2020). Closure of universities due to Coronavirus Disease 2019 (COVID-19): impact on education and mental health of students and academic staff. Cureus, 12(4). https://dx.doi.org/10.7759%2Fcureus.7541

120. Schworm, S. K., Cadin, L., Carbone, V., Festing, M., Leon,

E., & Muratbekova-Touron, M. (2017). The impact of international business education on career success — Evidence from Europe. European Management Journal, 35(4), 493-504. https://doi.org/10.1016/j.emj.2017.02.009

121. Sharma, S. K., Palvia, S. C. J., & Kumar, K. (2017). Changing the landscape of higher education: From standardized learning to customized learning. Journal of Information Technology Case and Application Research, 19(2), 75-80. https://doi.org/10.1080/15228053.2017.1345214

122. Sharma, S. P., & Singh, R. (2018). Buckling up the one belt one road (OBOR) initiative: Intentions of China and Ramifications for India. FOCUS: Journal of International Business, 5(1), 1-13. http://52.172.152.24/index.php/FJIBJPI/article/view/182096/169356

123. Sleeter, C., & Carmona, J. F. (2017). Un-standardizing curriculum: Multicultural teaching in the standards-based classroom. Teachers College Press.

124. Stevens, S., Mills, R., & Kuchel, L. (2019). Teaching communication in general science degrees: highly valued but missing the mark. Assessment & Evaluation in Higher Education, 44(8), 1163-1176. https://doi.org/10.1080/02602938.2019.1578861

125. Thatcher, A., Zhang, M., Todoroski, H., Chau, A., Wang, J., & Liang, G. (2020). Predicting the Impact of COVID-19 on Australian Universities. Journal of Risk and Financial Management, 13(9), 188. https://doi.org/10.3390/jrfm13090188

126. Thematic.Software. (2019). Thematic Analysis Software: How It Works & Why You Need It. https://getthematic.com/insights/thematic-analysis-software/

127. Thyroff, A. E., & Kilbourne, W. E. (2017). Understanding pro-environmental intentions through growth, competitiveness, and concern. Australasian Marketing Journal (AMJ), 25(2), 97-105. https://doi.org/10.1016/ j.ausmj.2017.04.005

128. Toquero, C. M. (2020). Challenges and opportunities for higher education amid the COVID-19 pandemic: The Philippine context. Pedagogical Research, 5(4). https://doi.org/10.29333/pr/7947

129. Tran, L. T., & Vu, T. T. P. (2018). Beyond the 'normal' to the 'new

possibles': Australian students' experiences in Asia and their roles in making connections with the region via the New Colombo Plan. Higher Education Quarterly, 72(3), 194-207. https://doi.org/10.1111/hequ.12166
130. UNECE. (2018). Bringing Standardization in University Curricula: Making the case. United Nations Economic Commission for Europe. https://www.unece.org/fileadmin/DAM/trade/Publications/ECE_TRADE_440.pdf
131. Valos, M. J., Maplestone, V. L., Polonsky, M. J., & Ewing, M. (2017). Integrating social media within an integrated marketing communication decision-making framework. Journal of Marketing Management, 33(17-18), 1522-1558. https://doi.org/10.1080/0267257X.2017.1410211
132. Verger, A., Steiner-Khamsi, G., & Lubienski, C. (2017). The emerging global education industry: analysing market-making in education through market sociology. Globalisation, Societies and Education, 15(3), 325-340. https://doi.org/10.1080/14767724.2017.1330141
133. Wan, C. D., Chapman, D., Hutcheson, S., Lee, M., Austin, A., & Md. Zain, A. N. (2017). Changing higher education practice in Malaysia: the conundrum of incentives. Studies in Higher Education, 42(11), 2134-2152. https://doi.org/10.1108/LHT-03-2018-0036
134. WorldBank.org/BRI. (2018). Belt and Road Initiative. World Bank. https://web.archive.org/web/20190219015644/http://www.worldbank.org/ en/topic/regional-integration/brief/belt-and-road-initiative
135. WVU/IMC.611. (2020). IMC 611: Marketing Research and Analysis. West Virginia University. https://marketingcommunications.wvu.edu/academics/ms-integrated-marketing-communications/marketing-research-and-analysis
136. WVU/IMC.612. (2020). IMC 612: Audience Insight. West Virginia University. https://marketingcommunications.wvu.edu/academics/ms-integrated-marketing-communications/audience-insight
137. WVU/IMC.613. (2020). IMC 613: Brand Equity Management. West Virginia University. https://marketingcommunications.wvu.edu/academics/ms-integrated-marketing-communications/brand-equity-management
138. WVU/IMC.615. (2020). IMC 615: Creative Strategy and Execution. West Virginia University. https://marketingcommunications.wvu.edu/

academics/ms-integrated-marketing-communications/creative-strategy-execution

139. WVU/IMC.616. (2020). IMC 616: Direct and Digital Marketing. West Virginia University. https://marketingcommunications.wvu.edu/academics/ms-integrated-marketing-communications/direct-and-digital-marketing

140. WVU/IMC.618. (2020). IMC 618: PR Concepts and Strategy. West Virginia University. https://marketingcommunications.wvu.edu/academics/ms-integrated-marketing-communications/pr-concepts-and-strategy

141. WVU/IMC.619. (2020). IMC 619: Emerging Media and the Market. West Virginia University. https://marketingcommunications.wvu.edu/academics/ ms-integrated-marketing-communications/emerging-media-and-the-market

142. WVU/IMC.Capstone. (2020). Capstone. West Virginia University. https://marketingcommunications.wvu.edu/learning-experience/capstone

143. WVU/What.Is.IMC?. (2020). What is IMC?. West Virginia University. https://marketingcommunications.wvu.edu/academics/ms-integrated-marketing-communications#whatcontainer

144. Zhang, M. M., Xia, J., Fan, D., & Zhu, J. C. (2016). Managing student diversity in business education: Incorporating campus diversity into the curriculum to foster inclusion and academic success of international students. Academy of Management Learning & Education, 15(2), 366-380. https://doi.org/10.5465/amle.2014.0023

145. Zhao, Y., & Gearin, B. (2016). Squeezed out: The threat of global homogenization of education to creativity. In Creative intelligence in the 21st century. Brill Sense.

146. Zhao, J., & Ferran, C. (2016). Business school accreditation in the changing global marketplace: A comparative study of the agencies and their competitive strategies. Journal of International Education in Business, 9(1), 52-69. https://doi.org/10.1108/JIEB-02-2016-0001

Contact information

Name of the author: Dr. Jason Lee Carter, DBA

Affiliation (University): City University of Macau, Taipa, Macau Assistant Professor, International Business Cohort (IBC), Faculty of Business

Email: jlcprofessional@gmail.com

Exponential Growth in Corporate Innovation: A Synergy of Big Data, Cloud Computing & Digital Technologies

Deepak Kumar Dash & Sonny Dhamayana

Abstract

More and more, we unleash the value of Data in each walk of life, we recognize the true potential of it, which is supplemented by technological breakthrough. This progress has redefined Innovation. Thereby influencing the socioeconomics of the society, we live in. The corporate world has taken the path of innovation through digital transformation, leveraging the value of Open-Source platforms and thereby being a part of the Innovation Eco-System. The recent pandemic COVID-19 outbreak, which started at the beginning of 2020 or arguably later part of 2019 (thus the name), became an accelerator towards Industry 4.0 transformation. The pandemic has made society, governments, industry bodies, private and public bodies, and social not-for-profit entities to be more agile and change to adapt to various scenarios without having much time to prepare. Thankfully digital disruptions and new dimension technologies are available to explore and get solutions thereof. World economic forum envisages 'an estimated 70% of new business value created over the next decade will be based on digitally enabled platform business models'[1]. 10th Sustainable Goal, as defined by the United Nations which is 'Reduce inequality within and among countries' focuses on the unequal distribution of power, wealth, and social instability. The emerging technologies have the potential to have a positive impact on the inequality front and create a better value for every global citizen. Entities need to use data and ever-evolving digital technologies to generate that value through innovation and collaboration through socioeconomic business models. This paper takes a deep dive into the synergy of the digital technologies on corporate innovation which

is growing at an exponential rate, which business entities across scale and size are adopting or in other words, are made to adopt, for the core reason of survival. And the mantra is business innovation with the pandemic, not post, as it's going to stay long.
Keywords: INSaaS , Insight as a Service, Corporate Innovation

JEL Classification: O33, O35, Q55

"Everything we do during and after this crisis [COVID19] must be with a strong focus on building more equal, inclusive and sustainable economies and societies that are more resilient in the face of pandemics, climate change, and the many other global challenges we face."
António Guterres, SecretaryGeneral, United Nations

1. Introduction

Technologies can bring enormous benefits to the lives of people irrespective of their social status. There are numerous successful implementations of current generation technologies and the value it generated over the last decade or so is well noted. However, many of this technology deployment remains at an early stage. There is a concern that automation, AI, robotics will perform more and more human-oriented jobs gradually if not immediately and these technologies will create a greater divide in society and countries based on skill level. A world of haves and have nots will widen. The value and challenges related to the emerging technologies are discussed below sections. A structured approach is made to discuss corporate innovation followed by key technologies and the impact thereof on the digital economy with an eye on (with) pandemic scenarios.

1.1 Innovation

MIT defines 'Innovation as the process of taking ideas from inception to impact'[2]. Moreover, the concept also suggests the difference between 'Innovation' and 'innovation'. Big 'I' innovation focuses on large efforts flowing from research and development, whereas small 'i' innovation focuses on more innovative behaviors across an organization. Closed

Innovation used to be a successful innovation model, which lost its significance with the Open Innovation model.

1.1.1 Innovation Ecosystem

Then comes Innovation Ecosystem (iEco). Merriam Webster defines 'ecosystem as the complex of a community of organisms and its environment functioning as an ecological unit'[3]. The innovation ecosystem is a community of stakeholders who are responsible for bringing the impactful innovation onboard, bear in mind the outcome may result in a profit or may not. One of the key aspects of the innovation ecosystem is the innovation loop. Each activity is translated as an Experiment and culminates as an Evaluation or Lessons learned.

1.1.2 Corporate Innovation

Not only adapting to the new normal but also anticipating and being prepared for the COVID-19 type situations purely from the survival or business as a usual point of view, organizations are required to prepare themselves and thankfully we have emerging technologies supporting almost all industries, powered by the new fuel i.e. DATA. Collaboration across solutions are current and future game-changers in coming years. As per research by McKinsey, 'By 2025, digital ecosystems could account for about 30% of global corporate revenue'.[4] As a part of building Smart Home Strategy, Artificial Intelligence lead payers like Amazon, Apple, Google, and the Zigbee allied to explore and exploit the business value which is going to explode in times to come.

1.1.3 Technological Innovation

Many innovation models do not involve technology, but their dependency on information and communication largely affects the business value. Online platforms deliver many a need of today's urban life entertainment (Netflix, amazon prime, etc.), home delivery of groceries, home appliances, medicines, etc. for example. The recent pandemic opened another dimension of online education and tele counseling by doctors, hearing of judicial cases, etc. to name a few. Recent advancements have already created spaces for SaaS(Software as a Service-Microsoft Office

365 for example), Paas(Platform as a Service-Google apps engine for example), IaaS(Infrastructure as a Service-Amazon AWS product for

example), and many cloud providers as well. A platform is a business model wherein business entities connect, interact and drive value. 'Nearly 70% of the value to be created in the next ten years will be based on business models that are digitally enabled'[5], as studied by World Economic Forum. Innovative business models equipped with tech support are there to create value and build resilience. COVID-19 underpinned the touchless and online aspects of the business. The Organization for Economic Co-Operation and Development's Science, Technology and Industry Scoreboard 2017 reported that the '50 largest R&D performers account for 40% of all business R&D efforts in Canada and the US, and more than half of such efforts in Germany and Japan'.[6]

1.2 Digital Ecosystem

Beyond doubt, today's businesses are Customer-centric and the use of digital technologies in everyday life is normal and in other words not being part of digital is somewhat not normal. The ecosystem is a set of interconnected services when it comes digital.

1.2.1 Digital Transformation of Business and Organizations

Irrespective of the industry sector, Industry 4.0 has reshaped value, agility, and adaptability. According to McKinsey & Company, 'an emerging set of "digital ecosystems" modeled after firms like Facebook and Airbnb could account for more than $60 trillion in revenue by 2025, or more than 30% of all global corporate revenue'.[7] According to a study published by Accenture, '62% of consumers say their purchasing consideration is driven by a company's ethical values and authenticity, and 74% want more transparency on companies' stances on environmental and social issues, and on how they source their products and ensure safe working conditions'.[8] While nearly '96% of organizations are in some phase of transformation'[9], according to research firm IDG, and '90% of enterprises have already adopted a "digital-first" business strategy'[10].

"As we enter a new age of technology, the world remains reliant on a 160 yearold industry, whose core mission is to responsibly and efficiently stay

ahead of tomorrow's energy demand. At ADNOC, we call this mission 'Oil and Gas 4.0.' 'Oil and Gas 4.0' means rethinking how our industry adopts and applies technology, connects with nontraditional partners, shows environmental leadership and most importantly attracts and retains talent." Dr. Sultan Al Jaber, MD & CEO, ADNOC Group

2. Material and Methods

A detailed literature search was conducted in electronic databases through Google search engine and scholarly articles were used for broader searches. 'United Nations Conference on Trade and Development, Technology and Innovation Report 2021'[11] was studied in depth. 'Organization for Economic Co-operation and Development reports and libraries related to Digital Economy'[12] were investigated and corresponding data and statistics were gathered. 'Massachusetts Institute of Technology, Corporate Innovation model on Innovation Ecosystem'[13] is discussed. 'Investment interests in technologies were studied through PitchBook quarterly reports on various technologies'[14]. The last search was conducted on 28th May 2021. Required citations and references have been made across the paper in respective sections. 'Publication and Patent search data were retrieved from Elsevier's Scopus database of academic publications and Patseer database for the period 1996-2018. Market size data, as measured by the revenue generated, is based on various online market research reports. Since each market research report yields somewhat different numbers, the market size data was collected so that the compound annual growth rate (CAGR) was the largest'[15]. From a visualization point of view, the yearly market size was considered.

2.1 Innovative Technology: Buzz Words

Emerging Technology, Frontier Technology, Disruptive Technology, and Exponential Technology are buzz words. New technologies, which are either recently being developed, underdeveloped or getting, developed in near future are emerging technologies. Moreover, the investment for research and development inclination is towards such technologies. 'Frontier technologies can disrupt or have the potential to disrupt the status quo of human society, alter the way people live, and lead to entirely new products and services'[16]. 'Disruptive technologies are innovations that drastically change the way organizations and industry's function'[17].

Exponential technology is those innovations that continue to advance exponentially, with disruptive economic and lifestyle effects. 'Moreover, exponential technologies are those whose current price-performance makes it feasible to incorporate them into today's business and social problems in new and previously impossible ways. '[18]

2.2 Technology Discussion

Whatever the word as mentioned above prefixed to technology may be, all of them refer to the same innovative technologies, which are creating a rippled effect in society and business domain. These are Internet of Things (IoT), Artificial Intelligence and Machine Learning (AI & ML), Big data, Blockchain, 5G, 3D Printing, Robotics, Drones, Gene Editing (CRISPR), Nano Technology and Solar Technology, Augmented and Virtual Reality, Quantum, and Edge Computing.

In the Model and Data section, we are providing visualization on the knowledge base, market size, key providers, and major industries along with various key indicators and performances related to each of the technologies backed by research-driven data.

Figure 1. ***Market Size of Frontier Technologies***

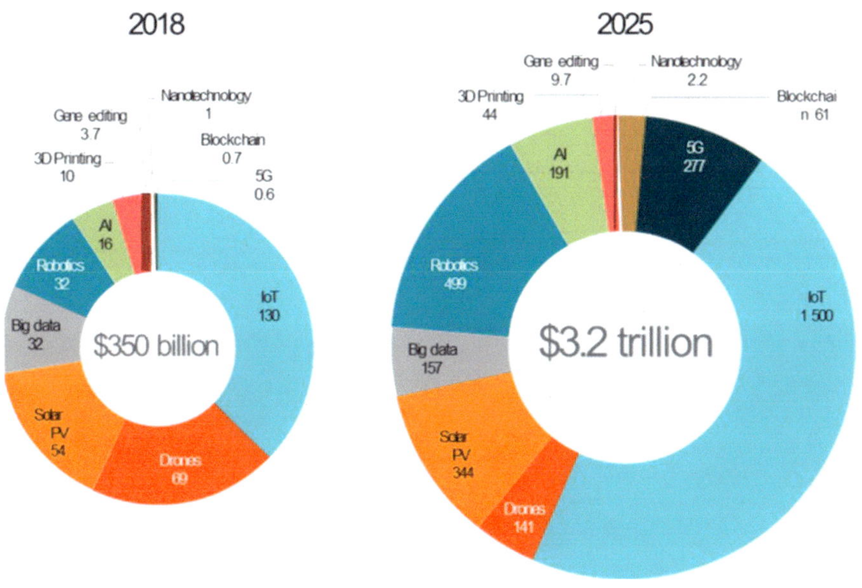

Source: UNCTAD Technology and Innovation Report, 2021

The market size of Technologies in terms of $billions

The $350-billion market of 2018, could grow to over $3.2 trillion by 2025, from these technologies.

2.2.1 Internet of Things (IoT)

More than device-to-device communication through the internet, it's about an intelligent network that can be controlled and managed by sensors and has the architecture of 3 layers. Perception, Network, and Application layer. This is otherwise termed as Internet of Everything. IoT, sensors come first that often comes with inbuilt microchips. As an NFC (Near Field Communication) tool 1st generation RFID (Radio-frequency identification) works on the principle of electromagnetic energy absorption and transmits simple, unique codes. Routers are the endpoint devices. As per Pitchbook 'IoT software market to reach $120.0 billion in terms of end-user spending in 2021, with much of this spending driven by the monitoring software provided by industrial automation incumbents'[19]. Vehicles on the road can talk to each other and the human-oriented accidents will be a matter of past, that's an example of devices being connected and similarly, sensor data is captured by the traffic department for better management. Given Covid situation and downward phase the auto industry is going through such Vehicle to Vehicle (V2V) or Vehicle to Infrastructure (V2X) techs can prove to be a real boon. Smart city, transportations, lightings, smart transportations, homes, etc. are more of connected devices set up. IoT growth is mainly driven by 'rising demand for advanced consumer electronics, the increasing adoption of smart devices and internet-enabled devices, the rise of telehealthcare services, and the emergence of automation technology in various sectors, even though cybersecurity, privacy concerns'[20], and skill availability negate the growth to some extent.

Figure 2. ***Number of Installed IoT Devices from 2015 2025***

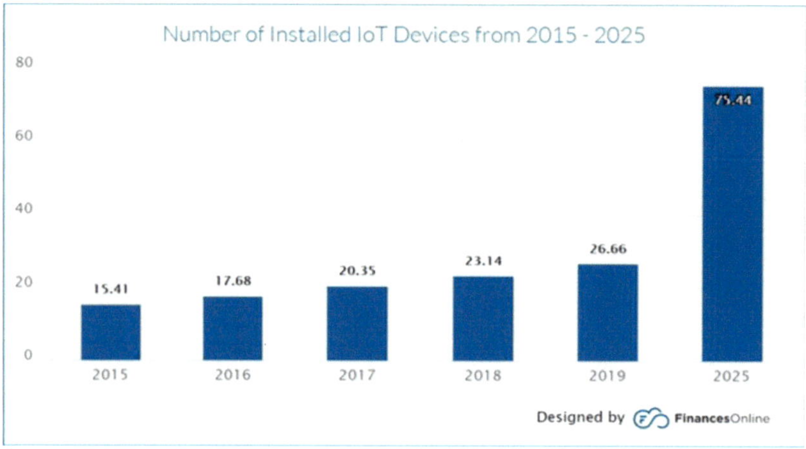

Source: FinanceOnline

2.2.2 Artificial Intelligence & Machine Learning (AI & ML)+ IOT+ AIOps

'AI is normally defined as the capability of a machine to engage in human-like cognitive activities. New implementations of AI are based on machine and deep learning and harness big data'[21]. AI applications hosted in the cloud environment are demonstrating better value when it comes to industrial AI. As Gartner reported in Nov 2020, on edge AI, 'over 10% of machine vision devices will have edge AI capability by 2024, led by machine vision cameras. Such business transactions are a classic case of Collaboration for technological value derivation. The timing and potential impact of edge AI technologies as well as the ethical aspect of AI must be understood to achieve competitive advantage and differentiation'[22]. Main service providers are from the US and off-late Europe and Middle East has also shown some leading players in the AI field. AI market growth is mainly augmented due to open source advancement in deep learning, image processing, investment flow, varied use cases solution, etc., however, a factor of restraint is the ethical AI aspect. The AI-related job market is growing at an exponential rate.

Figure 3. ***Business Value Forecast by AI Type***

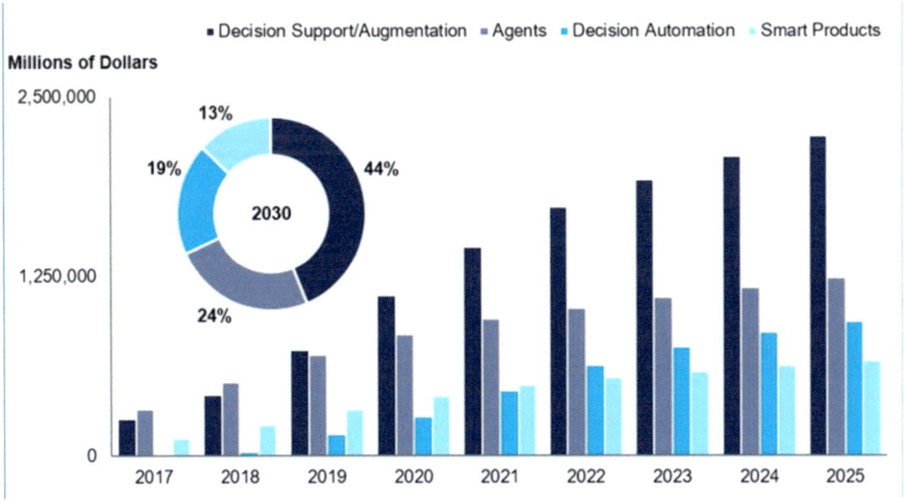

Source: Gartner 386366

2.2.3 Big Data (AI & ML)

Big Data involves transactions of datasets that have huge volume, variety, velocity, veracity, value, and complexity. 'Like AI and IoT, Big Data R&D is also dominated by the USA and China'[23]. The growth is mainly driven by more and more cloud services adoption, mobile devices, and apps launch, however, the business value awareness is not translated properly along with security and privacy concerns remain some hindering factors. A skilled workforce remains a challenge here.

2.2.4 Cloud & DevOps

A synergy of software Developers into Operations, build high-quality right to the need applications and address the scalability as well. DevOps scope includes communications and collaboration tools across the enterprise along with zero code or low code automated task processing bots like Robotic Process Automation. Recent investments are taking an inclination towards this emerging tech. In today's COVID-19 situation DevOps powered communication and collaboration tools, support feedback loop which plays a critical role as working from home has become a new normal. APIs are playing a vital role in the integration of systems. DevOps in the cloud environment has been drawing the attention of investors, citizen developers, and other corporates as such. 'Early-stage startups, such as Lightrun, are focused on building integrations with other developer tools to improve the ability to gather disparate log information and increase observability. Hyperscalers are also focused on the opportunity with the launch of Amazon's DevOps Guru in December, and incumbent Splunk launched an observability suite in October'[24].

2.2.5 Blockchain +AI

'A blockchain refers to an immutable time-stamped series of data records supervised by a cluster of computers not owned by any single entity'[25]. The blockchain serves as the base technology for cryptocurrencies, enabling peer-to-peer transactions that are open, secure, and fast. Offering payment solutions is a key part of the Fintech sector. Many investments are flowing into the companies offering payment solutions. As per the Deals monitoring platform Pitchbook, 'VC funding into payment fintech companies maintained its strong growth in 2020 with $11.7 billion invested across 773 deals—up 17.0% from 2019 and a record high. Toast was hit hard from COVID-19 lockdowns and had to reduce almost half of its staff just shortly after closing its Series F. However, the shift to delivery and takeout has helped drive growth opportunities, and we expect the company could go public in 2021'[26]. Consumer Finance is another area that covers day-to-day financial services like following savings and current account transactions, debit, credit, and other card transactions and even POS (point of sales) products, digital banking, and digital wallets.

2.2.6 3D Printing

3D printing, also known as additive manufacturing, produces three-dimensional objects based on a digital file. 3D printing can create complex objects using less material than traditional manufacturing. Currently, an entry-level 3D printer can cost as little as $200, while a top-notch industrial printer could cost more than $100,000. Of late, there has been a major shift in the filament or 3D printing material from plastic to metal and many cases concrete as well. The growth of this market is driven by different types of filaments, an increase in production speed reduced errors, and lesser time in delivering the printed object. More and more industries like healthcare, consumer electronics, automotive, dentistry, food, fashion, and jewelry are adopting 3D printed items. A skilled workforce is a challenge in this technology.

2.2.7 Robotics

Robots are programmable machines that can carry out actions and interact with the environment via sensors and actuators either autonomously or semi-autonomously. They can take many forms: disaster response robots, consumer robots, industrial robots, military/security robots, and autonomous vehicles. 'Primarily the USA is driving the growth of the robotic industry whereas many robot manufacturing companies are spread across the globe'[27]. Discrete manufacturing, process manufacturing, and resource industries are top industries of robots' usage. Skilled engineers are not freely available for this technology as well.

2.2.8 Drones

A drone, also known as an unmanned aerial vehicle (UAV) or unmanned aircraft systems (UAS), is a flying robot that can be remotely controlled or fly autonomously using software with sensors and GPS. Drones have been often used for military purposes, but they also have civilian uses such as in videography, agriculture, and delivery services. 'Top industries on drones are utilities, construction, and discrete manufacturing. Primary growth is driven by digitization, technological improvements in cameras, multidimensional mapping software, and sensory applications. The top three drone job locations are the United States, China, and France'[28].

2.2.9 Gene Editing

Gene editing, also known as genome editing, is a genetic engineering tool to insert, delete or modify the genome in organisms. Potential applications include drought-tolerant crops or new antibiotics or medical genomics. 'USA and China are driving the R&D in this space'[29]. The modest growth in this industry which is propelled by more investment flows and improvement in genetic engineering is constrained by medical and healthcare ethical concerns. Increase demand for genetically modified crops and synthetic genes are driving the demand. Medical scientists and biomedical engineers are the primary jobs and the demand is increasing.

2.2.10 5G + IOT

5G networks are the current generation of mobile internet connectivity, offering download speeds of around 1-10 Gbps (4G is around 100 Mbps) as well as more reliable connections on smartphones and other devices. Important components of 5G are network equipment and chips. 5G market ($608 million in 2018) is expected to more than double every year until 2025. Cost of infrastructure set up is a hinder on the growth.' Growth is driven by rising demand oadband, the growing use of smartphones and smart wearable devices, and the increase in mobile video adoptfor mobile brion, as well as rapid developments in IoT and the rising number of connected devices, initiatives towards smart cities, and shift in consumer preference from premise to cloud-based solutions. By 2035, global 5G value chain, will support 22 million jobs'[30].

2.2.11 Nanotechnology

Nanotechnology is a field of applied science and technology which deals with the manufacturing of objects in scales smaller than 1 micrometer. Nanotechnology is used to produce pharmaceuticals, commercial polymers, and protective coatings and to design computer chip layouts. Growth is driven by requirements for miniaturization of a wide range of devices but concerns related to environmental, health, and safety risks, as well as nanotechnology commercialization among global players, remain a constraint.

2.2.12 Solar Technology

Solar technology transforms sunlight into direct current electricity using semiconductors within Photo Voltaic (PV) cells. 'Chinese companies lead the solar PV market'[31]. Residential, commercial, and utility providers are major industries. The solar PV job market growing but uncertainties remain, and there is little evidence of a hiring boom.

2.2.13 Quantum Computing

Quantum computing, which stores information in quantum bits rather than a binary series. Many large corporates like Google, IBM, and Rigeti are trying their supremacy in quantum computing.

Figure 4. ***Who Could Create Value with Quantum Computing?***

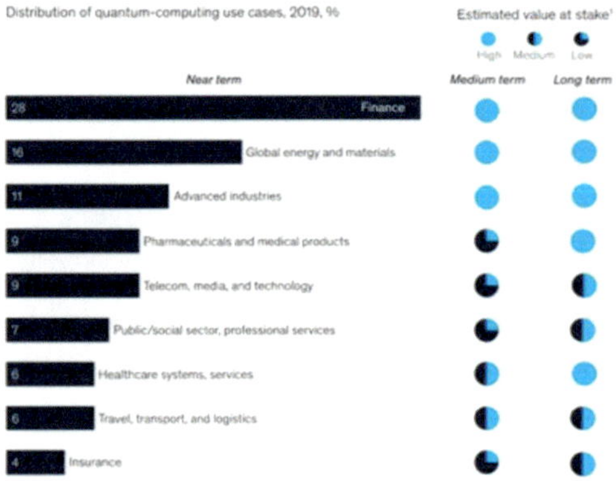

Source: McKinsey and Company

2.2.14 Virtual and Augmented Reality

Virtual reality (VR) and Augmented reality (AR) are complementary technologies to each other. The VR users are virtually transported, via headgear, to a virtual world while with AR, a superimposed layer is presented on the real world on a virtual monitor. The combination of AR and VR is called mixed reality (XR). Many industrial applications are driving the growth here.

3. Model and Data

Based on the available search results the datasets are analyzed and visualizations are presented.

Figure 5. ***The amount of Knowledge Invested in Each Technology. AI/ML with the Highest Publications and Patents During the Period of 1996 to 2018***

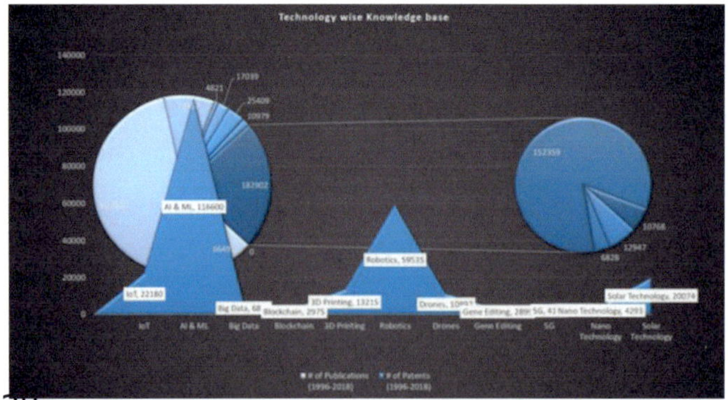

Source: DKD et.al for the current paper.

Figure 6. ***Technologywise Lead Providers and Lead Industries in Terms of Early Adoption of the Technology***

Technology	IoT	AI & ML	Big Data	Blockchain	3D Printing	Robotics	Drones	Gene Editing	5G	Nano Technology
Major Players	Alphabet	Alphabet	Alphabet	Alibaba	3D Systems	ABB	3D robotics	CRISPR therapeutics	Ericsson	Agilent
	Amazon	Amazon	Amazon Web Services	Amazon Web Services	ExOne Company HP	KUKA	Parrot	Editas	Huawei (network)	BASF
	Cisco	Apple	Dell Technologies	IBM	Stratasys	FANUC	Yuneec	Horizon Discovery	Nokia	Samsung
	IBM	IBM	HP Enterprise	Microsoft		Mitsubishi	Boeing	Intellia	ZTE	Intel
	Microsoft	Microsoft	IBM	Oracle		Hanson Robotics	Lockheed martin	Precison	Huawei (chip)	
	Oracle		Microsoft	SAP		Softbank Robotics			Intel	
	PTC		Oracle						MediaTek	
	Salesforce		SAP						Qualcomm	
	SAP		Splunk						Samsung Electronics	
			Teradata							
Top 3 Industries(Early adoption)	Consumer	Retail	Finance	Finance	Manufacturing	Manufacturing (Discreet)	Utility	Biotech	Utility	Manufacturing
	Finance	Finance	Manufacturing	Manufacturing	Healthcare	Manufacturing (Process)	Construction	Agrigenomics	Manufacturing	Pharmaceuticals
	Healthcare	Manufacturing	Professional services	Retail	Education	Resource	Manufacturing	Research	Public Safety	Energy

Source: DKD et.al for the Current Paper

Below observations were made from the data gathered from Enterprise Venture Capital Investment Statistic Organization for Economic Co-operation and Development (OECD). We look at the data from the VIC (Venture Investment Capital) Value for the digital economy across country- wise and year-wise with positive growing impact and outliers if any.

Figure 7. ***Anomaly VIC Value in the Year 2018 to 2019***

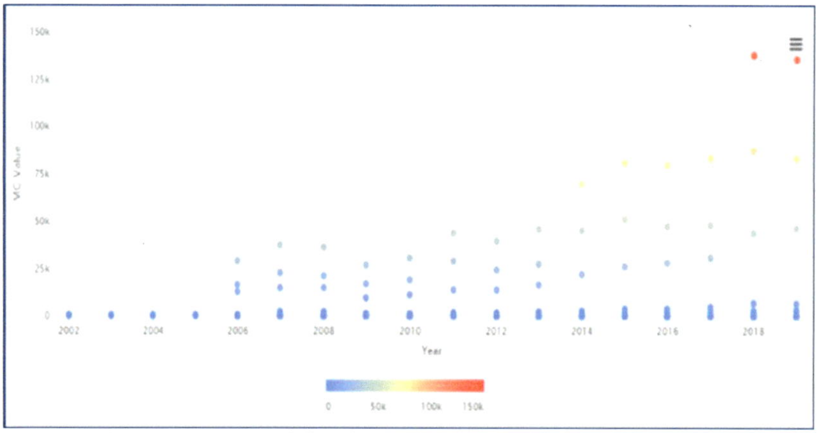

Figure 7. Source: DKD et.al for the Current Paper

4. Results and Discussion

The growth of the emerging technologies is bound to be multiplied manyfold each passing year because more and more data is available which in turn helps to improve the technical know-how. IoT and IIoT

Figure 8. ***Value Against Countries, that USA Gives the Big Impact in VIC Value Distribution Among the Other Country, it Means Investment is Flowing Mostly from This Country***

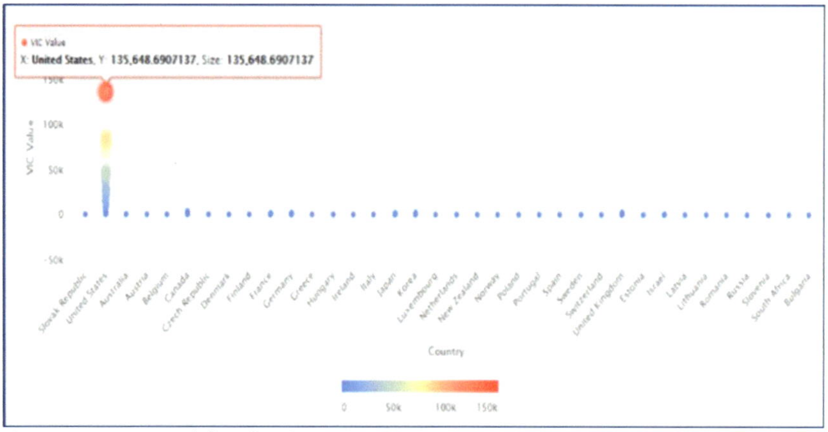

Source: DKD et.al for the Current Paper

(Industrial Internet of Things) are going to be the game-changer while exponential progress in the field of AI and Deep Learning, 3D printing, and 5G are already shaking society. While the positive values of all the technologies are well understood, the risk factors associated with data privacy, cybersecurity remain other challenges. During the current COVID-19 pandemic, AI and big data have been used for screening patients, monitoring the outbreak, tracking and tracing cases of the disease, predicting its evolution, assessing infection risks, and developing vaccines, etc. Innovation-oriented startups can get early funding if they choose to solve real-world problems using the discussed technologies, which holds a greater promise, in post-COVID-19 days. 'Some sectors making good progress with the combination of discussed emerging technologies are the Mobility sector, Agriculture and Biotechnology sector, Supply chain sector, and Wellness sector'[32]. Complementing, supplementing, and bringing the synergy on board are the technologies discussed here, which in turn contribute towards the exponential surge in terms of innovation and growth opportunity for corporates.

5. Conclusion

We are almost 18 months old to face the wrath of COVID-19, and as the economy shows recovery businesses need not only disaster preparedness but also opportunity preparedness which is a byproduct of this pandemic. Post pandemic economy will be a boom time for the digital economy and companies who are driven by data. 'Economists at Goldman Sachs see the U.S. economy growing a stellar 8% in 2021, and the IMF pegs 2021 growth at 6% globally—6.4% in the United States, and a stunning 12.5% in India. JPMorgan Chase CEO Jamie Dimon's 2021 shareholder letter predicts a multiyear boom. However, this growth wave is tightly coupled with a profound and comprehensive move to "online everything." The faster the market moves, the more you rely on data to anticipate and adjust. At the core of every innovation and opportunity, data provides the why and the how'[33]. This research allowed us to understand the economic impact of the synergy created by emerging technologies through big data in the cloud computing environment. More and more innovative ways to collaborate among emerging technologies are the way forward for exponential economic growth.

6. References and bibliography

Citation of a journal paper/website/online libraries

1. Akman, P., Whiting, K., Torkington, S., Mazhari, A., Colondam, V., & Kolaczkowski, M. (n.d.). Shaping the Future of Digital Economy and New Value Creation. World Economic Forum. https://www.weforum.org/ platforms/shaping-the-future-of-digital-economy-and-new-value- creation#:~:text=An%20estimated %2070%25%20of%20new,remain%2 0unconnected%20to%20the %20internet.

2. Budden, P., & Murray, F. (2019, October). An MIT Approach to Innovation: eco/systems, capacities & stakeholders. https:// innovation.mit.edu/assets/BuddenMurray_An-MIT-Approach-to-Innovation2.pdf.

3. Ecosystem and Its Components. (2017). In ScienceAid. Retrieved Jun 4, 2021, from https://scienceaid.net/Ecosystem_and_Its_Components
4. Boudet, J., Gregg, B., Rathje, K., Stein, E., & Vollhardt, K. (2019, July

8). The future of personalization--and how to get ready for it. McKinsey & Company. https://www.mckinsey.com/business-functions/ marketing-and-sales/our-insights/the-future-of-personalization-and-how- to-get-ready-for-it.

5. Akman, P., Whiting, K., Torkington, S., Mazhari, A., Colondam, V., & Kolaczkowski, M. (n.d.). Shaping the Future of Digital Economy and New Value Creation. World Economic Forum. https://www.weforum.org/ platforms/shaping-the-future-of-digital-economy-and-new-value- creation#:~:text=An%20estimated %2070%25%20of%20new,remain%2 0unconnected%20to%20the %20internet.

6. OECD Science, Technology and Industry Scoreboard 2017. (2017). OECD Science, Technology and Industry Scoreboard. https://doi.org/ 10.1787/9789264268821-en

7. Catlin, T., Lorenz, J.-T., Nandan, J., Sharma, S., & Waschto, A. (2018, February 20). Insurance beyond digital: The rise of ecosystems and platforms. McKinsey & Company. https://www.mckinsey.com/industries/ financial-services/our-insights/insurance-beyond-digital-the-rise-of- ecosystems-and-platforms.

8. Accenture. (1970, December 4). Majority of Consumers Buying From Companies That Take A Stand on Issues They Care About and Ditching Those That Don't, Accenture Study Finds. Newsroom. https:// newsroom.accenture.com/news/majority-of-consumers-buying-from-companies-that-take-a-stand-on-issues-they-care-about-and-ditching-those-that-dont-accenture-study- finds.htm#:~:text=Today%2C %2062%20percent%20of%20consumers,co mpany's%20ethical %20values%20and%20authenticity.

9. Dold, D., & Mies, H. (n.d.). Business Transformation : Succeeding in Disruptive Times. https://assets.kpmg/content/dam/kpmg/ch/pdf/brq-business-transformation-en.pdf.

10. Author: John Milburn Follow @ClearSkyeInc John Milburn is CEO at Clear Skye, & Milburn, A. J. (n.d.). What's Slowing Down Your Digital Transformation? 3 Questions to Ask. Business 2 Community. https://

www.business2community.com/strategy/whats-slowing-down-your-digital-transformation-3-questions-to-ask-

02401565#:~:text=While%20nearly%2090%25%20of%20businesses,do %20so%20successfully%20(IDC).

11. Technology and Innovation Report 2021. UNCTAD. (n.d.).(Full report) https://unctad.org/page/technology-and-innovation-report-2021.

12. OECD Science, Technology and Industry Scoreboard 2017. (2017). OECD Science, Technology and Industry Scoreboard. https://doi.org/ 10.1787/9789264268821-en

13. Budden, P., & Murray, F. (2019, October). An MIT Approach to Innovation: eco/systems, capacities & stakeholders. https:// innovation.mit.edu/assets/BuddenMurray_An-MIT-Approach-to-Innovation2.pdf.

14. Reports & Analyst Content: PitchBook. Venture Capital, Private Equity and M&A Database. (n.d.). https://pitchbook.com/news/reports.

15. Technology and Innovation Report 2021. UNCTAD. (n.d.).(page no. 122) https://unctad.org/page/technology-and-innovation-report-2021.

16. UNESCAP. (n.d.). Frontier Tech for SDG- . https://www.unescap.org/ sites/default/files/publications/Frontier. https://www.unescap.org/sites/ default/files/publications/Frontier %20tech%20for%20SDG.pdf.

17. EMERGING TECHNOLOGIES VS. DISRUPTIVE TECHNOLOGIES. (n.d.). https://www.ironmountain.com/blogs/2019/emerging-technologies-vs- disruptive- technologies#:~:text=Disruptive %20technologies%2C%20however%2C% 20are%20innovations,shares %20or%20fall%20into%20irrelevancy.

18. What is Exponential Technology? XponentialWorks. (2019, March 11). https://xponentialworks.com/what-is-exponential-technology/.

19. (n.d.). PitchBook Emerging Tech Report: Internet of Things (IoT). https://pitchbook.com/news/reports/h2-2020-emerging-tech-research-internet-of-things.

20. Technology and Innovation Report 2021. UNCTAD. (n.d.).(page no. 111) https://unctad.org/page/technology-and-innovation-report-2021.

21. Technology and Innovation Report 2021. UNCTAD. (n.d.). (page no. 110) https://unctad.org/page/technology-and-innovation-report-2021.
22. Goodness, E. (n.d.). Review of Emerging Technologies: Research Roundup for Edge Ai as a Platform for Growth. Retrieved from https://

www.gartner.com/en/documents/3995473/emerging-technologies-research-roundup-for-edge-ai-as-a-
23. Technology and Innovation Report 2021. UNCTAD. (n.d.). (page no. 112) https://unctad.org/page/technology-and-innovation-report-2021.
24. Reports & Analyst Content: PitchBook. Venture Capital, Private Equity and M&A Database. (n.d.). https://pitchbook.com/news/reports.
25. Technology and Innovation Report 2021. UNCTAD. (n.d.).(page no. 113) https://unctad.org/page/technology-and-innovation-report-2021.
26. Reports & Analyst Content: PitchBook. Venture Capital, Private Equity and M&A Database. (n.d.). https://pitchbook.com/news/reports.
27. Technology and Innovation Report 2021. UNCTAD. (n.d.).(page no. 116) https://unctad.org/page/technology-and-innovation-report-2021.
28. Technology and Innovation Report 2021. UNCTAD. (n.d.). (page no. 117) https://unctad.org/page/technology-and-innovation-report-2021.
29. Technology and Innovation Report 2021. UNCTAD. (n.d.). (page no. 118) https://unctad.org/page/technology-and-innovation-report-2021.
30. Technology and Innovation Report 2021. UNCTAD. (n.d.). (page no. 114) https://unctad.org/page/technology-and-innovation-report-2021.
31. Technology and Innovation Report 2021. UNCTAD. (n.d.). (page no. 120) https://unctad.org/page/technology-and-innovation-report-2021.
32. Reports & Analyst Content: PitchBook. Venture Capital, Private Equity and M&A Database. (n.d.). https://pitchbook.com/news/reports.
33. Merritt, D. (2021, May 5). Commentary: Data-driven companies will get more bang for the post-pandemic boom. Fortune. https://fortune.com/ 2021/05/05/post-covid-economic-boom-tech-transformation-data- cybersecurity/.

Citation of images

Figure 1. Technology and Innovation Report 2021. UNCTAD. (n.d.). https:// unctad.org/page/technology-and-innovation-report-2021

Figure 2. Number of IoT Connected Devices worldwide. (n.d.). https://financesonline.com. photograph. https://financesonline.com/number-of-internet-of-things-connected-devices/

Figure 3. https://www.gartner.com/en/documents/3868267/forecast-the-business-value-of-artificial-intelligence-w.
Figure 4. Distribution of Quantum Computing. (n.d.). photograph. https://www.mckinsey.com/business-functions/mckinsey-digital/our-insights/a-game-plan-for-quantum-computing.

Contact information

Name of the author: Deepak Kumar Dash, MBA,
PMP Affiliation (Workplace): Founder, DGTAL.AI Inc.
Email: d@dgtal.ai

Big Data for Small & MediumSized Enterprises

Joy Weigand

Abstract

This paper outlines the challenges that European small and medium-sized enterprises (SMEs) face in considering the use of Big Data, new technology and innovation. The meta-analytical methodology was used on data from Elsevier's Scopus data. A small corpus of six articles focusing on small and medium-sized enterprises in the European context were examined to shed light on the challenges faced by SMEs when considering the use of Big Data. The results show a number of internal and external factors. Internal factors related to management and their psychological preparedness of management supporting a culture of open-mindedness related to using the new technologies or knowledge in the use of the new technologies and finances such as available capital for equipment or tools or personnel. External factors included available external funding, stakeholder relations, and current legislation. Finally, this research adds to current research by providing a synthesis of information on the main challenges faced by SMEs in the use of Big Data.

Keywords: SMEs, Big Data, management considerations

JEL Classification: M10, M21, C89

Introduction

The recent explosion of technology that allows us to access large amounts of information, Big Data, has broadened possibilities and expanded opportunities for many big businesses. The technologies behind big data are revolutionizing business processes, approaches, strategies and has caused quite a disruption in the way business is conducted. Large, global, multinational corporations with a multitude of resources of various types, including financial and human resources, have the capabilities of very easily mining, managing, storing and exploiting the available volumes of data.

Taking advantage of the new technology and tools involved requires the ability to understand the prevailing and evolving concepts as well as the current practices which are constantly undergoing changing. Further, we see a high demand for technically trained staff by large companies and corporations with the ability to be able to afford the necessary talent and/or train staff to help companies and corporations use the data to gain a competitive advantage.

When referring to technology coupled with innovation, we often encounter the term, disruption. There are many forms of disruption including the disruption related to innovation introduced by Christensen et al. (2006). There is also digital disruption and societal disruption. There is no doubt that the recent pandemic, the outbreak of COVID-19, is a societal disruption that has had an effect on all types of companies in numerous forms. During the pandemic there were a number of changes in behavior leading to unexpected results. In the third quarter of 2020, for example, not only did bankruptcies increase, but also the registration of new businesses providing hope for the economy. The figure below shows the registration of businesses and the declaration of bankruptcies in the European Union (EU) from the first quarter

Figure 1. ***Registration of Businesses and Declaration of Bankruptcies in the EU***

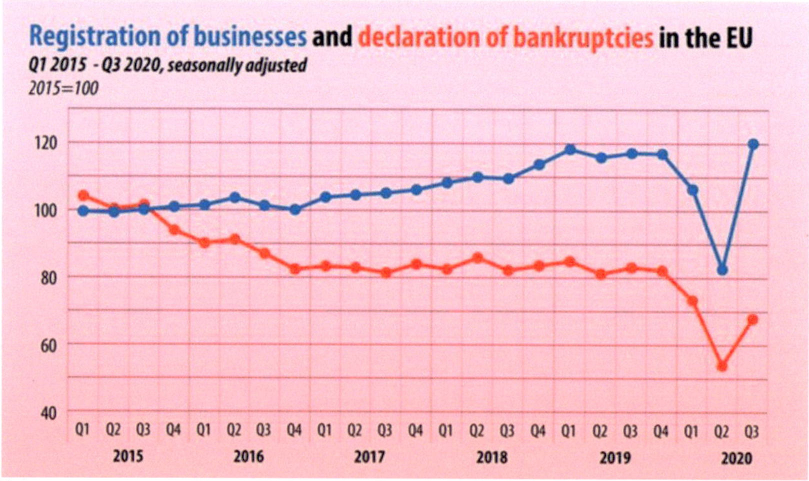

Source: EC.europe.eu Eurostat

of 2015 to the third quarter of 2020. The data is based on the absolute number of registrations and bankruptcies sent to Eurostat, the statistical office of the European Union, on a voluntary basis by some EU and European Free Trade Associate (EFTA) Member States (Eurostat, 2021, May 8).

This shows how important this one event has been a disrupting factor which has not only changed how we do business but also whether some businesses could exist to do any business at all. Many of the positive outcomes could be attributed to how successful companies could make some form of digital transformation, capitalizing on available technologies or transforming their business strategies.

So, what can we learn from the pandemic? According to researchers at Singapore Management University, Harvard University and INSEAD, "new entrants with digital operating models established exponential growth trajectories that greatly weakened or destroyed incumbents with fixed capacities" (George, et al., 2020). Some of these "new entrants," companies with short histories were SMEs. There were tech companies like ZOOM and Slack. Interesting, companies that did well were not only tech companies, like companies offering digital payment services. Successful companies came from a variety of sectors like home improvement, remote fitness, health and beauty products, grocery delivery services, and an array of many other home delivery services. What these companies had in common is that they were able to use the technology to quickly adapt to the changing demands of their customers or quickly create innovative business strategies to reach a larger customer base.

In times of crises as well as in times of stability, Big Data can help businesses understand the current situation moreover what further direction is necessary to enhance or broaden their business strategy. The question is: What challenges are SMEs facing with implementing strategies using Big Data? This is the question this paper attempts to answer. In order to understand the answers, clearly defined terms are needed to avoid confusion.

What is the meaning of Big Data?

There is no consensus on the definition of Big Data. The words 'big' and 'data' appeared together as Big Data around the 1990's when John Mashey from a Silicon Valley graphics company that dealt with large amounts of data, is quoted as saying "I was using one label for a range of issues, and I wanted the simplest, shortest phrase to convey that the boundaries of computing keep advancing" (Lohr, 2013). Since then, we have learned more about the characteristics of Big Data than the definition.

De Mauro, et al. (2016) argue for a definition including Big Data's 'informational asset' nature, specific 'characteristics' that should include 'technology' and 'analytical methods' used. Examining the first component, 'informational asset', anyone working in information science or asset management has probably come across Ackoff's hierarchical model from 1989, now known as the DIKW Pyramid, shown in Figure 2.

Figure 2. *DIKW Pyramid*

Source: Wikipedia

Figure 2. *Revised DIKW Pyramid*

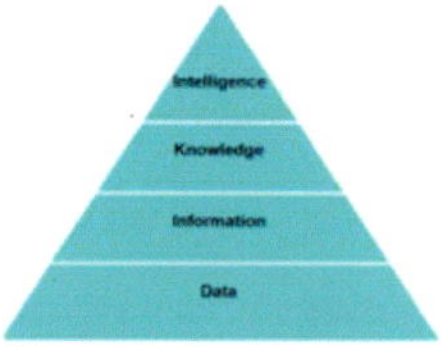

Source: the Author

According to Ackoff (1989), Data are valueless symbols that are the products of observation; information inferred from data is transformed into what is contained in descriptions; knowledge is know-how acquired by learning which is transformed into instructions; and wisdom is characterized by an increase in development. Ackoff (1989) also makes the distinction between intelligence and wisdom stating "intelligence is the ability to increase efficiency" and "wisdom is the ability to increase effectiveness." Keeping this in mind, I would argue that a new pyramid should have intelligence at the head of the pyramid containing completely automated processes with wisdom as the human aspect outside the pyramid, thus resulting in the pyramid seen in the Figure 3.

Table 1. *Big Data Vs*

Number	Year	V	Definition	Source
1	2001	Variety	...no greater barrier to effective data management will exist than the variety of incompatible data formats, non-aligned data structures, and inconsistent data semantics.	[3,5]
2	2001	Velocity	E-commerce has also increased point-of-interaction (POI) speed and, consequently, the pace data used to support interactions and generated by interactions.	[3]
3	2001	Volume	E-commerce channels increase the depth/breath of data available about a transaction (or any point of interaction).	[3]
4	2013	Validity	...is the data correct and accurate for the intended use.	[1, 4, 5, 6, 8]
5	2013	Value	How to determine the prescriptive value of data?	[1, 2, 4, 7, 8, 9]
6	2013	Variability	Many options or variable interpretations can confuse interpretation.	[1, 2, 5, 7, 9]
7	2013	Veracity	... to the biases, noise and abnormality in data.	[1, 2, 4, 6, 8, 9]
8	2013	Viability	... can the data be analyzed in a way that makes it decision-relevant?	[2, 5]
9	2013	Virility	... Defined by some users as the rate at which the data spreads; how often it is picked up and repeated by other users or events.	[9]
10	2013	Viscosity	... used to describe the latency or lag time in the data relative to the event being described.	[9]
11	2013	Visibility	... the state of being able to see or be seen – is implied.	[4, 8, 5]
12	2013	Visualization	Making all that vast amount of data comprehensible in a manner that is easy to understand and read. With the right analyses and visualizations, raw data can be put to use otherwise raw data remains essentially useless.	[7]
13	2013	Volatility	... how long is data valid and how long should it be stored.	[5, 6]
14	2014	Vagueness	... confusion over the meaning of big data (Is it Hadoop? Is it something that we[']ve always had? What[`]s new about it? What are the tools? Which tools should I use? Etc.)	[1]
15	2014	Venue	... distributed heterogeneous data from multiple platforms, from different owner[`]s systems, with different access and formatting requirements, private vs. public cloud.	[1]
16	2014	Vocabulary	... schema, data models, semantics, ontologies, taxonomies, and other content- and context-based metadata that describe the data[`]s structure, syntax, content, and provenance.	[1]
17	2015	Vincularity	... it implies connectivity or linkage.	[5]
18	2015	Visible	We live in an increasingly visual world and the statistics of increase in the number of images and videos shared on the Internet is staggering.	[5]
19	2015	Vitality	... criticality of the data is another concept that is crucial and is embedded in the concept of Value.	[5]

Source: Cartledge, 2016

As early as the point at which data becomes information, De Mauro et al. (2016) would label this an 'informational asset'.
By way of describing the characteristics, mostly beginning with the letter V, a working definition of Big Data can be derived. An analyst by the name of Doug Laney is generally credited with describing Big Data in terms of volume, variety and velocity. Volume pertaining to data with a quantity greater than terabytes or petabytes. Variety relates to the type and nature of the data not merely structured data, but semi-structured data in addition to unstructured data, as technologies have progressed to be able to process such data. And velocity refers to the interaction speed. Many more characteristics have been added over time, mostly beginning with the letter
V. According to Chuck Cartledge (2016), in the table below with sources in Appendix A, there were about 19 characteristics beginning with V that were counted at that time.
Referring to 'specific technology' related to Big Data, it can be classified into the following domains: storage, analytics, mining and visualization. These are some of the specific technologies that should be included when referring to Big Data.
Analytical methods in Big Data are numerous and continually emerging and evolving. Some of the prevailing methods are cluster analysis, genetic algorithms, natural language processing, machine learning, neural networks, predictive modelling, regression models, social network analysis, sentiment analysis, signal processing and data visualization.
Combining these various components, De Mauro et al. (2016) thus arrive at the definition: "Big Data is the information asset characterized by such high volume, velocity and variety to require specific technology and analytical methods for its transformation into Value."

Why is Big Data important in business?

Competitive advantage is what companies seek and Big Data can deliver competitive advantage. Companies want to be agile enough to be able to make quick real-time decisions based on the most accurate information possible. When companies can collect, store, manage, analyze information about stakeholders, use the tools and devices to communicate with customers, clients and business partners leveraging the many of the Vs: Volume, Validity, Veracity, etc., this provides for the best positioning in increasingly competitive business environments. Further, this has already been determined by digital start-ups and large corporations.

What is an SME?

Each political system has determined the definition of small and medium-sized enterprises (SMEs) or small and medium-sized businesses (SMBs) both of which from here on will be referred to as SMEs. In the context of the European Union, the European Commission has defined an SME "as having less than 250 persons employed, an annual turnover of up to EUR 50 million, or a balance sheet total of no more than EUR 43 million" (European Commission, 2003). Medium enterprises are companies employing 50-249 persons. Small enterprises can be further broken down into small vs. micro where the former is composed of companies employing 11-49 persons and latter is composed of companies employing less than 10 persons. Small, micro, and medium-sized enterprises for the purposes of this paper, will be aggregated.

Why are SMEs important to the European economy?

The economy is fueled by SMEs. In Europe, they are known as the background of the European economy because they are often responsible for providing a number of jobs, important for the mental health of citizens and they also directly and indirectly provide economic health for countries in terms of stimulating growth.

According to the Organization for Economic Co-operation and Development (OECD) there are a multitude of reasons why SMEs are important (Guerría, 2021):

"Small and medium-sized enterprises (SMEs) and entrepreneurship are essential drivers of economic and social well-being. Representing 99% of all businesses, generating about 60% of employment and totaling between 50% and 60% of value added in the OECD area, SMEs are key for delivering sustainable and inclusive economic growth. They are instrumental to ensure that our economies and societies adapt to major transformations, such as digitalization, globalization, ageing and environmental pressures."

SMEs are necessary for the economy.

The next section will show the method used to answer the main research question related to the challenges faced by SMEs with regard to Big Data.

Material and Methods

A meta-analysis was performed on articles from Elsevier's Scopus. Scopus is an abstract and citation database containing nearly 36, 377 titles from peer reviewed journals, book series and trade journals. A search for articles containing 'Big Data' and 'SMEs' within the title was conducted in May 2021. This returned 455 papers. This filtered data was then cleaned up by removing entries which did not cover the geographical space of European Union, where the paper was irrelevant or unrelated to the topic or where the paper relied on secondary data. Filtering the search yielded six papers.

Results and Discussion

Issues that SMEs faced when tackling Big Data related to the implementation or transitioning into using digital technologies for business. SMEs often run into the "obstacle related with decision-makers' lack of awareness concerning digital technologies potential and implications" (Azevedo & Almeida, 2021). Lack of awareness was not the only obstacle faced by SMEs. Michna and Kmieciak (2020) cite "having a culture of open-mindedness, managers supporting knowledge-sharing and the company's financial condition" as factors related to willingness of SMEs to implement technological advances.

Focusing particularly on the SME healthcare sector, Hogan, et al. (2018) found that European SMEs in healthcare can succeed or fail depending upon factors related to region, , business model, size, stage of evolution, financial structure and legal form with further country-specific factors including the economic environment, and structural factors such as cultural norms.

The factors reported by Çera et al. (2019) were divided into three categories: internal resources (financial, inability to find new potential partners, difficulties in the acquisition of new technologies or innovation), institutional environment (political, economic social, legislative, ecological and technological issues), and psychological motives (lack of motivation and delegation of responsibilities).

Factors that could be a "potential barrier to big data analytics in SMEs" are the inability to "afford sophisticated computer systems where the costs outweigh the benefits or in-house capabilities for the selection, installation, configuration and maintenance of complex IT systems" according to Soroka et al. (2017).

Obstacles, according to Coleman, et al. (2016) include lack of understanding, dominance of domain specialists, cultural barriers and intrinsic conservatism, shortage of in-house data analytic expertise and bottlenecks in labor market. According to Brzozowska (2008) there were three categories of entrepreneurial factors financial (capital position, positive/negative cash flow, understanding of cash flow principles), managerial (experience, skilled, clear/fragmented vision, attitude) and strategic (coherent or unclear plan, market position/approach, stakeholder relations or operating independent).

To summarize the results, they can be clustered into two categories external and internal challenges. External challenges were regional, economic, social, legislative, ecological and/or market.

Figure 4. ***External challenges SMEs face implementing big data***

Source: the Author

There were also internal challenges which fell into the following domains: legal, financial, technological, psychological and managerial. Legal related to the legal form of the enterprise. Financial meant the costs outweighed the benefits. Technological challenges involve having the right expertise. Psychological challenges related to preparedness. Managerial concerned the practices of management.

Figure 5. ***Internal challenges SMEs face implementing big data***

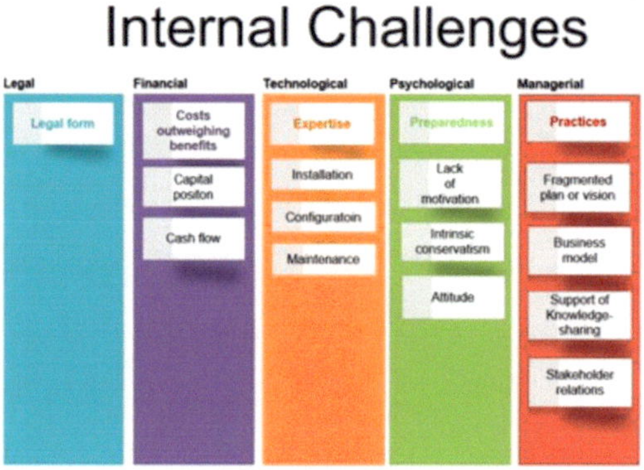

Source: the Author

There are many challenges that SMEs faced when deciding whether to use Big Data, to implement new technologies, to transition to digital strategies.

Conclusion

SMEs face many internal and external challenges when implementing big data and digital transformational strategies. There must be conducive regional, economic, social, market, ecological and legislative environments supporting SMEs in the implementation of big data strategies. In order to gain a competitive advantage, SMEs need to internally be psychologically prepared to support a culture of open-mindedness towards technology, support knowledge-sharing, adjust their business plans to utilize financial and technological resources working with different stakeholders if necessary to implement big data strategies.

References and bibliography

1. 1. Ackoff, R., 1989. From data to wisdom. Journal of applied systems analysis, 16(1), pp. 3-9.

in SMEs-A Training Course Geared towards Decision-Makers. Educational Sciences, 11(4), p. 151.

3. Brzozowska, K., 2008. Business angels in Poland in comparison to informal venture capital market in European Union. Engineering Economics 57(2).
4. Cartledge, C., 2016. How many Vs are there in Big Data. working paper. 18 February.
5. Çera, G., Belas, J. & & Zapletalíková, E., 2019. Explaining business failure through determinist and voluntarist perspectives. Serbian Journal of Management.
6. Christensen, C., Baumann, H. & Ruggles, R. &. S. T., 2006. Disruptive innovation for social change. s.l.:Harvard business review, 84(12), 94.
7. Coleman, S. et al., 2016. How can SMEs benefit from big data? Challenges and a path forward. Quality and Reliability Engineering International, 32(6), pp. 2151-2164.
8. Commission, E., 2003. Commission Recommendation of 6 May 2003 concerning the definition of micro, small and medium-sized Enterprises, s.l.: Official Journal of the European Union.
9. De Mauro, A., Greco, M. & & Grimaldi, M., 2016. A formal definition of Big Data based on tis essential features. Library Review.
10. George, G., Lakhani, K. & Puranum, P., 2020. What has changed? The Impact of Covid Pandemic on the Technology and Innovation Management Research Agenda. Journal of Management Studies, 2020 December, pp. 1754-1758.
11. Guerría, A., 2021. Organisation for Economic Cooperation adn Develoment (OECD). [Online] Available at: https://www.oecd-ilibrary.org/sites/75974c58-en/index.html?itemId=/content/component/75974c58-en [Accessed 15 May 2021].
12. Hogan, D., van Kranen, H. & & Morré, S., 2018. Optmising SME potential in modern healthcare systems: Challenges, opportunits and policy recommendations. Public health genomics, 21(1-2), pp. 1-17.
13. Laney, D., 2001. 3D data management: Controlling data volume, velocity and variety. META group research note, 6(70), p. 1.
14. Lohr, S., 2013. Bits. [Online] Available at: https://bits.blogs.nytimes.com/2013/02/01/the-origins-of-big-data-an-etymological-detective-story/ [Accessed 15 May 2021].

15. Michna, A. & & Kmieciak, R., 2020. Open-Mindedness Culture, Knowledge-Sharing, Financial Performance, and Industry 4.0 in SMEs. Sustainability, 12(21), p. 9041.
16. Soroka, A., Liu, Y., Han, L. & & Haleem, M., 2017. Big data driven customer insights for SMEs in redistributed manufacturing. Procedia CIRP, 63, pp. 692-697.

Big Data Vs References

[1] Kirk Borne, Top 10 big data challenges - a serious look at 10 big data vs, https://www.mapr.com/blog/top-10-big-data-challenges-%E2%80%93-serious- look-10-big-data-v%E2%80%99s, 2014.
[2] Seth Grimes, Big data: Avoid 'wanna v' confusion, https:// www.informationweek.com/big-data/big-data-analytics/big-data-avoid-wanna-v-confusion/d/d-id/1111077?, 2013.
[3] Doug Laney, 3d data management: Controlling data volume, velocity and variety, META Group Research Note 6 (2001).
[4] Rob Livingstone, The 7 vs of big data, http://rob-livingstone.com/2013/06/ big-data-or-black-hole/, 2013.
[5] Rajiv Maheshwari, 3 vs or 7 vs - whats the value of big data?, https:// www.linkedin.com/pulse/3-vs-7-whats-value-big-data-rajiv-maheshwari, 2015.
[6] Kevin Normandeau, Beyond volume, variety and velocity is the is-sue of big data veracity, http://insidebigdata.com/2013/09/12/beyond-volume-variety- velocity-issue-big-data-veracity/m 2013.
[7] BI Sta_, Why the 3vs are not su_cient to describe big data, https:// datafloq.com/read/3vs-sufficient-describe-big-data/166, 2013.
[8] University of Technology Sta_, The 7 vs of big data, http://mbitm.uts.edu.au/ feed/7-vs-big-data, 2013.
[9] Bill Vorhies, How many vs in big data the characteristics that define big data, http://data-magnum.com/how-many-vs-in-big-data-the-characteristics-that-define-big-data/, 2013. Source: Cartledge, 2016

Contact information

Name of the author: Joy Weigand, MBA
Affiliation (University): EDU Effective Business School
Email: workzajoy@hotmail.com

The Effect of Technological Changes on Women's Entrepreneurial Behavior (The Case of EBusiness in Nigeria)

Doris IkeOkereke. N

Abstract

The purpose of this study was to examine the effects of technological changes on human behavior. This study focused on Information Communication Technology (ICT), which facilitates data and artificial intelligence (AI) driven digital platforms, to review the effect on the entrepreneurial behavior of women entrepreneurs in Nigeria. Entrepreneurial behavior was studied in the context of new venture creation, entrepreneurial marketing, and self-directed learning. The descriptive qualitative study involved the interview of 6 women entrepreneurs who operated e-businesses using digital platforms in Nigeria. Existing literature was reviewed for secondary data. The study revealed that ICT encouraged women to create new ventures due to its low cost, convenience, and direct connection to the market. It also motivated the women entrepreneurs to compete by engaging in entrepreneurial marketing and self-directed learning. The study revealed poor connectivity, high cost of data, and constant changes in online technology as some of the challenges facing Nigerian women entrepreneurs in e-business.

Keywords: Business, Digital, Entrepreneurial behavior, Machine Learning, Women Entrepreneurship.

JEL Classification: M130, M150, D910

Introduction

The proliferation of information technology in societies has effectuated a paradigm shift in various sectors of the economy. Technology itself is defined as a manufactured system that utilizes knowledge and organization to create objects and techniques that support the realization of definite goals (Carroll, 2017). Technology exists in mechanical, medical, industrial, and communication sectors. However, the interest in this study is Information Communications Technology (ICT going forward), an aspect of technology that has gradually woven into the fabric of the daily lives of the average Nigerian citizen. ICT facilitated the data-driven digital platforms used for communication and information sharing. Constant developments have seen these platforms provide e-business support for enterprises in all areas. The development of Artificial intelligence (AI) and Machine learning (ML) used by the digital media facilitates information sharing in a way that influences strategic decision making and aids optimization of operational routine for businesses that are analytical and can describe data (Chalmers et al., 2020).

Internet availability in Nigeria has enabled various data-driven digital platforms that support multiple sectors in the economy. According to the Nigerian Communications Commission (NCC) (2021), compared to 450,000 connected fixed lines in the year 2000, Nigeria, with about 208.8 million residents, has 205,252,058 phone lines (107%, teledensity) as of September 2020, with an internet subscription at 151,512,122. ICT has been one of the most critical drivers of economic and social value in the last 50 years (Kunjlata, 2018), making it one of the predictors of economic efficiency.

Figure.1. ***Active Internet Subscription in Nigeria as of March 2021***

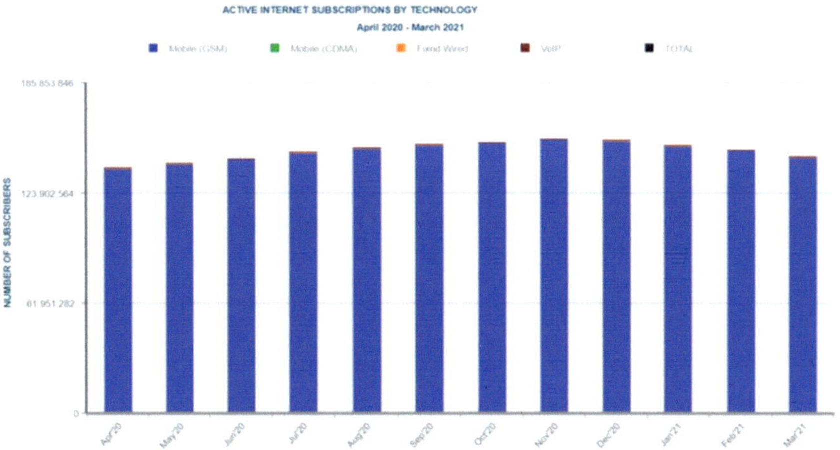

Source: Nigerian Communications Commission Report, 2021

The increase in internet usage in Nigeria is mainly due to its use by Nigerian businesses. The ease of access and cost-effectiveness attracts entrepreneurs to host their businesses on digital platforms. Companies with access to big data such as Facebook, Google, and Amazon deployed AI and ML to support enterprises with analytics, combined linguistic rule, and online recommendations (Whig, 2019). These features support marketing and customer engagement. This made e-business attractive for low investment entrepreneurs and low-income earners seeking multiple sources who engage mainly in trading, retailing, and service business. In the Nigerian Economy, these categories of people comprise mainly women entrepreneurs (Ukommi and Agha, 2016).

Before the emergence of the Global System for Mobile Communication (GSM) in 2000, business in Nigeria was primarily traditional. Women engaged in small-scale production, trading, and services. Nigerian Banking services were hardly automated, and micro-funding was not easy. Digital channels were not available for marketing. The diffusion of digital technology, advancement in algorithm abilities, access to richer data, and computing power brought in benefits such as cost-saving automated processes, improved productivity, human capital development, accumulation of credit scores through the use of e-wallets market access, and lower barriers to entry for business. These incentives consequently influenced the entrepreneurial behavior of entrepreneurs, especially women who are challenged by dual roles, low capital and access to market.

Entrepreneurial behavior can be defined as the behavior of individuals that fosters an ability to operationalize the concept of entrepreneurship through opportunity recognition, initiative, creativity, and risk management (Mulasari et al., 2019). This study views new venture creation, entrepreneurial marketing, and self-learning as activities that describe entrepreneurial behavior.

This paper brings a new perspective to the study of the impact of technology on women's entrepreneurship to ascertain how their entrepreneurial behavior is affected by changes in technology in the context of e-business. The study highlights the need to give attention to developing the infrastructure supporting the deployment of information communications technology in Nigeria to maximize the merits of women entrepreneurship to the nation. It will also highlight the benefits of ICT to women's entrepreneurship in Nigeria.

The following research questions served as a guide to investigate the effect of technological changes on women's entrepreneurial behavior in the e- business context;

1. Has new venture creation by women been influenced by changes in ICT?
2. How do changes in ICT through data-driven digital platforms influence the entrepreneurial marketing behavior of women entrepreneurs?
3. Has technology affected the entrepreneurial self-learning of women entrepreneurs?

Literature Review

Entrepreneurship

In the economic context, entrepreneurship is a catalyst for economic growth. Giriunine et al. (2016) defined entrepreneurship as a combination of capital, labor, and other resources to organize a business and undertake necessary risks to gain profit. The Global Entrepreneurship Monitor (GEM) defines Entrepreneurship as any undertaking by an individual or a group to create a new venture, modify or expand an existing one (Rusu and Roman, 2017). Entrepreneurs, through their various economic activities, drive economic growth. They drive competition, create employment and wealth through innovation (Stoica et al., 2020).

Although entrepreneurship has been studied generally, some scholars have highlighted some distinctions between male and female entrepreneurship. According to Shmailan (2016), female entrepreneurship is often characterized by less risk, less capital, and low debts and is less open to expansion than male entrepreneurship. In less developed countries, the divide between male and female entrepreneurs is more pronounced due to cultural influences on women. Women's entrepreneurship in Nigeria, which is more informal, is characterized by low investment, low assets, and poor managerial skills. The challenges to women entrepreneurship in Nigeria include gender stereotypes, family roles, poor access to funds, lack of supporting infrastructure, and access to market (Ukommi and Agha, 2016).

Technological Changes (Artificial Intelligence, Machine Learning) and Entrepreneurial behavior

In the course of entrepreneurship, entrepreneurs undertake purposeful activities fueled by their inherent characteristics to ensure success. Entrepreneurial behaviors exhibited by individuals focus on creating value through innovative processes, acquiring skills and knowledge to aid problem-solving and efficiency in business operations (Mulasari et al., 2019).

The nature and scope of entrepreneurial activities of e-business are influenced by digital technology through developments in areas such as (AI) and its component (ML). AI imitates human abilities, but its subset ML is programmed to teach itself how to learn and improve its performance. Machines can process data using adaptive algorithms to perform tasks requiring human intelligence (Chalmers et al., 2020).

Digital platforms driven by AI shape information that influence the entrepreneur's decision to create a new venture and expand existing ones. The AI in digital media highlights trends, market direction, customer behavior, and preferences using available data. The information provided by the AI in digital platforms promotes the entrepreneur's tendency to prospect and explore new business opportunities (Chalmers et al., 2020). Funding of small business ideas through micro credits facilitated by Fintech startups who offer micro credits based on the credit scores generated by scoring algorithms provides intermittent funding support for e-businesses (Strusani and Houngbonon, 2019).

Morris et al. 2002 seen in Sadiku-Dushi et al. (2019), defined Entrepreneurial marketing as the "proactive identification and exploitation of opportunities for acquiring and retaining profitable customers through innovative approaches to the risk management, resource leveraging and value creation." Machine learning algorithms on digital platforms provide the entrepreneurs with insights needed to target customers individually and enhances communication (Chalmers et al., 2020). It offers predictive analytics that provides insight into customer spending patterns, tastes, and preferences. This promotes marketing optimization.

In self-directed learning, the individual takes the initiative without external help to identify learning needs, seek out resources, material, and humans, and set self-evaluated learning goals. Before the arrival of the internet in Nigeria, self-learning avenues excluded data-driven digital platforms. Learning through available options such as paid training or books was challenged by access, time, and cost. An increase in the use of technology for education via the internet has amplified self-directed learning (Jaleel and Anuroof, 2017). Machine learning in digital platforms such as Coursera, through the predictive ability of its deep learning algorithm (Strusani and Houngbonon, 2019), supports skill acquisition, rich information sharing, opinion sharing, sentiment detection, raising awareness on emerging topics, recommends valuable skills to users based on detected interest thus driving self-learning.

Theoretical Underpinning

The expectation that changes in technology will affect the entrepreneurial behavior of women entrepreneurs who are digitally active was based on Bandura's social learning theory (1977) and Julian Rotter's Social learning theory (1954). Bandura built on Skinner's theory agreeing that external stimuli shape behavior. Thus changes in the external environment are responsible for changes in human behavior (Basri et al. 2020). According to Bandura's social learning theory, an individual's personality is a product of the interaction between behavior, psychological factors, and the environment.

Rotter's social learning theory stated that interactions with people in a meaningful environment determine human behavior (Edinyang, 2016). The above views emphasized the power of the environment in shaping human behavior. The technological environment, in this case, interacts with the individual and psychological factors to trigger entrepreneurial behaviors in the women entrepreneurs.

Research Method

The methodology used in this study to acquire primary data was the descriptive qualitative research method. The study participants were selected purposively based on the criteria that they operated their business on a digital platform. Six women entrepreneurs drawn from various industries were participants in the study. Primary data was collection was through an interview of the participants, while secondary data came from online library journals.

Results & Discussion

The 6 study participants (See Fig. 2 below) were interviewed to ascertain how the changes in ICT affected their entrepreneurial behavior, specifically in the area of new venture creation, entrepreneurial marketing behavior, and self-directed learning.

New Venture Creation. All but two of the participants were employed but saw opportunities in e-business which they took. They started their businesses to generate extra income. Participant 1 explained that she got her business idea on social media, contacted her distributors, and set up her online shop. According to her, it was convenient and cost-saving. Furthermore, the recent pandemic validated e-business more than ever. Participant 5 explained that without e-business platforms, her skincare business would not have taken off. It was the only option to market her products, given that she had a day job. Participant 2 said, "A significant reason that encouraged me to be a major distributor of the company I work with is ICT, the reason is that I know I can control and be in charge of my business from anywhere I am. Connect with customers, partners in several countries and run the business like we are in a physical office. ICT has made it easy to take stock, receive payments, confirm payments, send receipts, all I need to run an organized business".

Entrepreneurial Marketing: All the participants explained marketing as essential to success in e-business. They had to learn how to target their audience, create contents to attract them, package and present their products with attractive images and videos. Participant 5 explain the need to understand the social media algorithm and how to use hashtags. "I learned to create flyers, take pictures and create videos as marketing materials. Digital business challenges your creativity". Participant 1 said, "Other people are marketing similar products, you have to be creative, learn to connect and communicate with potential customers, you have to ensure your product is of good quality to avoid tarnishing your reputation." Participant 4 explained that her marketing drive was influenced by other entrepreneurs online. Observing others gave her the courage and confidence to learn how to market and engage an audience online. She was influenced to come live on Facebook to promote her agricultural products.

Selfdirected learning. Participant 3 learned the processes of making cosmetics online and got two certifications online in her line of business. Participant 1 explained that between Google and Youtube, there were enough materials and videos to teach almost anything. She explained, "I always have data so I can look up whatever I need to learn. The good thing is that you learn the skills for free ". Participant 5 learned photography, video editing, and graphics design online to use them for marketing. Participant 6 says, "once you have data, you can learn anything online, ask for directions, find suppliers and markets for your goods" .

Discussion

The availability of digital platforms facilitated by developments in ICT created a new business environment for small-scale female entrepreneurs. The interview conducted revealed that using the internet for business was a low- cost approach that directly connected the market. It was also easy for working women to set up new businesses to earn extra income. This agreed with Kirkley (2016) stating that technological advancements influenced new venture creation, given the emergence of digital platforms, which promoted markets, business network opportunities, and social demographic factors such as social trends in the use of products.

E-business requires networking, communication, constant promotion, and good customer service. The openness of the online environment encourages social comparison, which promotes a good performance. Verduyn et al. (2020) explained that operating in a technological and dynamic environment requires innovative marketing; thus, to remain profitable, female entrepreneurs who use digital platforms engage in creative marketing activities influenced by social learning and social comparison.

A few of the participants appreciated the need to understand the ML algorithm on social media. The need to move with trends and ensure good performance heightens the need for constant learning. Learning has become a part of the digital world such that female entrepreneurs find it natural to go online searching for knowledge and solutions. This aligned with Abbas et al. (2019) that social media platforms influence learning behavior, promoting education. The interview revealed a level of self-confidence on the part of the participants who proudly identified themselves as entrepreneurs while fostering their achievements in e-business.

Conclusion

This study aimed to examine the effects of technological changes on human behavior, and ICT was explicitly viewed as it affected the behavior of women entrepreneurs. After reviewing existing literature and an interview of 6 entrepreneurs, the study found that ICT influenced the decision to start new ventures. AI on digital platforms affected the marketing behavior and self- directed learning of women entrepreneurs. To a large extent, business today is driven by data. Businesses should strategically increase their digital footprints to capture the digital market. As indicated from the study, entrepreneurs and businesses need to acquire relevant skills and knowledge to run a digital business. Entrepreneurs require the skill to analyze digital data promoted by AI on digital platforms for informed and strategic decision- making. The use of marketing insights provided by ML analytics is vital for marketing optimization and should be embraced by entrepreneurs. The focus of the Nigerian government and support organizations should gear towards the provision of digital facilities that can support female entrepreneurs. Online entrepreneurship education platforms, data centers to support research and deployment of AI, entrepreneurship central information system, e-payment facilitation, better connectivity for enhanced data computation, and affordable data subscription are necessary to harness the potentials of the technological environment provided by e-business. Technology has provided a route for female entrepreneurs to express their creativity and achieve their goals.

Figure 2. ***Participants' Demographics***

Participants	Line of Business	Age	Academic qualification	Years in business	Digital Platforms
Participant 1	Distributorship of beauty products	37	Bachelors degree	3	Instagram
Participant 2	Education & Network Marketing	40	Higher Diploma	6	Facebook, WhatsApp
Participant 3	Manufacturing Cosmetics	47	Bachelors degree	4	WhatsApp, Facebook
Participant 4	Agro-processing	40	Bachelor in Technology	2	WhatsApp, Facebook
Participant 5	Manufacturing Cosmetics	40	Masters degree	3	Facebook, Instagram
Participant 6	Agriculture	41	Bachelor of Science	4	Facebook, Instagram

Source: the Author

Refreneces and Bibliography

1. Abbas, J., Aman, J., Nurunnabi, M., and Bano, S. (2019) The impact of social media on learning behavior for sustainable education: Evidence of students from selected universities in Pakistan.Sustainability. 11(1683). doi:10.3390/su11061683
2. Basri, H., Amin, S.,Umiyati, M., Mukhlis, H., Irvuani, r. (2020) Learning theory of conditioning. Journal of Critical Reviews. Vol. 7(8), 2024-2031. 197-1595100562.pdf (jcreview.com)
3. Carroll, L., L. (2017) A comprehensive definition of technology from an ethological perspective. Social Sciences. Vol. 6 (4), 126. https://doi.org/ 10.3390/socsci6040126
4. Chalmers, D., Mackenzie, N., G. And Carter, S. (2020) artificial intelligence and entrepreneurship: implications for venture creation in the fourth

industrial revolution. Entrepreneurship Theory and Practice. 0(0),1- 26. https://journals.sagepub.com/doi/pdf/10.1177/1042258720934581

5. Edinyang, S., D. (2016) The significance of social learning theories in the teaching of social studies education. International Journal of Sociology and Anthropology Research. Vol. 2(1), 40-45. The-Significance-of-Social-Learning-Theories-in-the-Teaching-of-Social-Studies-Education.pdf (eajournals.org)
6. Giriuniene, G., Giriunas, L., and Cernius, G. (2016) Identification research of the concept of entrepreneurship: The theoretical aspect. International Journal of Economics and Financial Issues. Vol. 6 (S6), 164. EconJournals.com
7. Jaleel, S. and Anuroofa, O., M. (2017) A study on the relationship between self directed learning and achievement in information technology of students at secondary level. Universal Journal of Educational Research. Vol. 5(10), 1849-1852. DOI: 10.13189/ujer.2017.051024
8. Kirkley, W.,W. (2016) Creating ventures: Decision factors in new venture creation. Asia Pacific Journal of Innovation and Entrepreneurship.Vol. 10(1), 151-167. DOI 10.1108/APJIE-12-2016-003
9. Mulasari, S., A., and Tentama, F., Subardjo, Sulistyawati, Kusuma, D., R., Sukesi, T., W. (2019) Entrepreneurial behavior in entrepreneurial pioneer in Ngalang village. International Journal of Scientific and Technology Research. Vol. 8(12), 2038-2045. http://www.ijstr.org/final-print/dec2019/Entrepreneurial-Behavior-In-Entrepreneurial-Pioneer-In-Ngalang-Village.pdf
10. Nigerian Communiction Commission (NCC), (2021). Challenges of technology penetration in an infrastructure deficit economy (Nigeria perspective) https://www.ncc.gov.ng/technical-regulation/research/956- challenges-of-technology-penetration-in-an-infrastructure-deficit-economy-nigeria-perspective
11. Nigerian Communiction Commission (NCC), (2021) Industry statistics and reports. https://www.ncc.gov.ng/statistics-reports/industry-overview#view-graphs-tables-5

12. Rusu, V., D. and Roman, A. (2017) Entrepreneurial activity in the EU: An empirical evaluation of its determinants. Sustainability. Vol 9(10), 1679. https://doi.org/10.3390/su9101679

13. Sadiku-Dushi. N., Dana, L., Ramadani, V. (2019) Entrepreneurial marketing dimensions and SMEs performance. Journal of Business Research. 100, 86-99. https://iranarze.ir/wp-content/uploads/2019/09/10039-English-IranArze.pdf
14. Shmailan AB (2016) Compare the characteristics of male and female entrepreneurs as explorative study. Journal of Entrepreneiurship and Organization Management.Vol 5(4). Doi: 10.4172/2169-026X.1000203
15. Stoica, O., Roman, A., and Rusu, V., D. (2020) The nexus between entrepreneurship and economic growth: A comparative analysis on groups of countries. Sustainability. 12(3), 1186. http://dx.doi.org/10.3390/su12031186
16. Strusani, D., and Houngbonon, G., V. (2019) The role of artificial intelligence in supporting development in emerging markets. International Finance Corporation, EMCompass. Note 69. https://www.ifc.org/wps/wcm/ connect/32e54505-3bfb-4198-b939-e1e8847715f1/EMCompass-Note-69- Role-of-AI-in-EMs.pdf?MOD=AJPERES&CVID=mNdPiNf
17. Ukommi, A., S., and Agha, E., S., (2016) Women Entrepreneurship in Nigeria:A Study of women in Uyo Metropolis. International Journal of Social Sciences. Vol.10 (4). http://socialscienceuniuyo.com/wp-content/ uploads/2017/04/Article-9-Ukommi-A.-S.-and-Agha-E.-O..pdf
18. Verduyn, P., Gugushvili, N., Massar, K., Taht, K., Kross, E. (2020) Social comparison on social networking sites. Current Opinion in Psychology. Vol. 36, 36-37. https://www.sciencedirect.com/science/article/pii/S2352250X20300464
19. Whig, P. (2019) Artificial intelligence and machine learning in business. International Journal on Integrated Education. Vol. 2(2), 64-68. https:// media.neliti.com/media/publications/334128-artificial-intelligence-and- machine-lear-cc5e833c.pdf

Contact information

Name of the author: Doris Ike-Okereke.N

Affiliation (University): LIGS University, Hawaii. USA.

Email: doris.iyke@gmail.com

How Synergy of Economics Skills and Educational Methodology Help Transforming through the Communication Crisis and Beyond

V. G. Biruk and CoAuthors

Abstract

This article has been writing in many years of research into the issues of risks and skills of anti-crisis management for various industries enterprises. It is based on the scientific and practical ability of convergence, economic, social, financial, and legal knowledge to develop information and communication technologies.

The article provides examples of LIGS University students who are specialists in industries from different countries who, in conditions of uncertainty, ambiguity, and lack of information, can transform the knowledge and skills collected into changing the behavior of people and business models. Furthermore, we provide evidence that using the acquired skills of crisis management, requiring good cross-disciplinary understanding and communication in a cross-cultural society, showing how cooperation between students and teachers in dissertation research can lead to scientific and practical solutions in the global industrial and digital era.

The scientific and practical article demonstrates the simplicity and availability of cross-disciplinary knowledge in the digital economy, which is a reasonable basis for the subject of Crisis Management to be attractive and easily adapted for the operational, tactical, and strategic activities of individuals or organizations.

JEL Classification: O33, H12, J24, I25, L80

Introduction

In the discussion of the researcher's role in the convergence of industrial and educational-scientific technologies in crises, we are going through the analysis of international trends in the implementation of the Industry 4.0 and 5.0 concepts and related problems: cybersecurity; management and education, economic and political behavior in the processes of transformation for enterprises and society.

The transformation of the industrial community into the post-industrial world, the digital era, and the economy of impressions, or formally speaking, the transition from the third technical revolution to Industry 4.0 then 5.0, has been taking shape with particular intensity decade. That is facilitating by the struggle for cyber sovereignty of countries and the aggressive competition of technology companies that increasingly absorb the spheres of politics, finance, economics, life on earth, and space.

The Dow Jones Index, for example, is a benchmark for market makers and speculators not only on Wall Street but also in all international financial markets today. It 80% formed, not by industrial corporations, as traditionally required by the global industry, but by High-Tech service companies.

In all management approaches, within massive automatization for economic and social activity, three categories are considered: legal, social, humanitarian, and financial and economic. Management models are like any other process. They are systematic and interact with any other methods or systems in a unique organization (company).

Most professionals, especially students, need economic knowledge and interaction models in their careers and study. Especially in the era of transition to a global, post-industrial economy and digital world. Learning about life and profession, all people, accumulating experience and qualifications, come to the need to transform this knowledge of value: for themselves, their families, and society. There is no more universal model for transforming knowledge of experience as educational methodologies through teaching, training, exchange and mentoring.

The teacher also cannot do without basic cross-disciplinary knowledge to help promote the necessary expertise among students, especially when the qualifications and reputation of the teacher grows.

The need is growing not only for improving one's qualifications but also for students and professors' research work and administration professionals.

Moreover, there is a great need to borrow knowledge from professionals in various fields. This convergence takes place best in the framework of postgraduate education, where students are professionals from different industries and cultures, models of society, and the mechanism of transformation. Like many of my colleagues, I appreciate with dignity eight years of work at LIGS University.

For the conversion of knowledge and skills, converted and generated in the cooperation of a professor and a student, it is most effective to use the delegation model. What does the exchange of the roles of lecturer and researcher, initiator of an idea, and performer mean?

I have tried this interaction mechanism many times to rehabilitate insolvent and bankrupt enterprises undergoing a reverse transformation. As a qualified specialist in anti-crisis management, by the decisions of the Supreme Arbitration Court, many enterprises or a financial organization were offered for management.

According to statistics of the Crisis Management Institute, accurately collected during the decades and annually analyzed and published, many years led by Dr. Larry L. Smith, a good friend of mine, more than fifty percent of all cases of crisis, catastrophic or bankruptcy loaded (linked with) by CEO, senior or line manager decision making. The reason, as we could guess, lies in the overvalued governing ambition of managers. Being enthusiastic and approved in personal competence qualified managers to sacrifice threats and weaknesses of the business operation and ignore controlling and disclosure requirements, many risks and consequences.

The author and co-authors of the concepts hope for the reader's understanding of the values of skills, the transformation of knowledge and behavior into effective changes to benefit all those interested in the educational and scientific process. And how the Anti-Crisis strategies can help professionals adopt innovations for efficiency and competitiveness purposes.

History and trends in Information Communication Technologies (ITC)

To understand the reasons for such a success of Hi-Tech in the conquest of the primary kind is no need to refer to the evolution of human development and its philosophy, which takes millennia. It is enough to analyze the period of three to four centuries, from households and the steam engine to the present day, contains the main secrets of such a transformation. Over the past two centuries, technological innovation has radically changed the business environment in many ways.

Industry 4.0 is the term used in the modern manufacturing world. Industry 5.00 is the revolution in which man and machine reconcile and find ways to work together to improve the means. The production efficiency is on the cusp is a popular name for the current trend of using technologies, such as the Internet of Things, Big Data, Cloud Computing, Robotics, and Artificial Intelligence (AI). To create more innovative, more productive, more resilient, and more adaptable factories and production processes.

The value created by Industry 4.0 in the race has to increase productivity and gain a competitive advantage. Manufacturers must embrace new digital industrial technologies included in a single value chain in the aggregate of the Internet of Things and digital manufacturing. They unite the physical and virtual worlds.

When explaining the international practice of introducing innovations, it should note that every country advanced in technology. Especially Japan, the USA, Israel, Singapore, Finland, and China are trying to use Hi-Tech to develop transnational corporations and entrepreneurial initiatives of their small and medium-sized businesses.

The main problems that have emerged and are increasingly affecting the industrial sector of countries, especially developing and countries with economies in transition, are the speed and criteria of such transformation. Analytics of the campaign's effectiveness for the trends of automation, robotization, digitalization, and artificial intelligence in the field of cognitive technologies. And the virtual world of business divides most of the industries of the industrial sector into two camps:

- Those that, having betrayed a significant financial and human resource to the victim, staying in the first car of technological progress. A caveat may be the fact that statistics 90% of corporations cannot withstand the costly race of transition from new to more advanced platforms;

-Those that did not recognize the taste of leadership and risk, not even getting into the last wagon, next to the 4.0 and 5.0 industry. Since the usual modernization of production does not solve the issue of acquiring competitive advantages, it remains a socially-oriented concept of development of the economy and industrial complex.
a socially-oriented concept of development of the economy and industrial complex.

How to transform ICT achievements to the contemporary education and scientific process?

In crisis and transformational circumstances, this knowledge must pass not only through the management but also through all team employees. Since not only the company or organization is under stress, but also the entire staff. Therefore, the practical principle of delegation in managing a process, project, or enterprise is also actively implemented in educational methodologies. Students, often on a pre-agreed topic, can and should play a lecturer's role or be opposed to their teacher.

So, within the framework of the MBA, DBA, and especially the Ph.D., we have repeatedly tested the capabilities and resources of the student and teacher in ensuring the effectiveness and quality of the research being carried out, mastering the set of necessary knowledge. For example, when having received several students in scientific direction for Ph.D. and DBA degrees at LIGS University, I had to spend three weeks working in a library in a suburb of Chicago working on my research. Same time my students, working in various fields of science and industry in many countries. At the same time, the students were happy to give lectures to develop my competence in specialist industry knowledge.

As proof of the convergence of economic and other knowledge into an educational methodology, then into skills and profession, I want to tell the story of several cases, using the example of working with students of LIGS University. Thanks to Alexandra Oravcova, one of the University managers, in 2013, she asked me to prepare for the Management course.

However, having practiced in governing for two decades and assessed the possibilities, especially the fact that there are already few places for innovations in classical management. That have been operating for more than fifty years without a system of significant changes, and I proposed a new, unprecedented for the Western and Eastern world, course "Anti-crisis management." Thus, the abbreviation or concept ACM (Anti-crisis Management) arose in Eastern European and Eurasia countries, which went through a long chain of political, economic, and social crises during the last three decades.

It is well known that the global business community has well adapted to existing technological management matrices and models developed in the twentieth century. That made it possible to cope with cyclical and counter-cyclical crises. However, what worked and set in the XX century becomes ineffective and even unacceptable in the XXI century.

Traditional management as a discipline and profession is losing its competitive advantages in crises, incredibly high risks, and uncertainty. In virtually and large-scale digitalization conditions, more and more services are required that provide cross-disciplinary skills and knowledge and the ability to change and learn in crisis conditions quickly. Publications and modern scientific research can judge the decrease in the importance of management. In recent decades, there has been the minimal progressive proposal of both operational and strategic management models. However, as all traditional industries succumb to the fashion of full automation, robotization and digital twins continue to use old management models.

Also, scientists and founders of management of the XX century today do not find and do not offer the proper concepts that can quickly adapt experienced managers in modern management changes associated with the growth of information and communication technologies. For example, even such a Guru of management and Competitiveness as Professor Michael Porter has not written about leadership in governing for the last 10-15 years, as I could guess. Instead, they were moving into the field of analysis of medicine management, political trends, and other modern concepts of scientific and practical direction.

The new post-industrial world and the digital era will require a fundamentally new management system associated with changes in products and services by introducing digital twins, artificial intelligence, 5G, and cloud technologies.

Those corporations that ensure the implementation of post-industrial systems show their greater efficiency and productivity with significant reliability, both of technological processes and equipment durability.

In international practice, the basic principles and rules of action after a disaster and unforeseen circumstances of the destruction of objects or systems, including software systems, are subject to the standards and methodology of the Business Continuity Institute. Together with some other institutions, are considered the basis of procedures for a crisis from disasters and destruction? Also, the international organizations as the Project Management Institute and Risk Doctor with its enthusiastic leader Dr. David Hillson, or substantial professional association as Insole Europe and Insole World. The American Bankruptcy Institute and the national economic regulation institutions have a well-developed methodology for bankruptcy procedures, resolving restructuring and reorganization of enterprises in a state of insolvency or their inefficiency.

However, there were no models of management of production and organizations in the procedure of a sudden severe crisis. The collapse of socialism and communism had become such a generator of anti-crisis methods, transformed into new management decisions, professions, and competencies—the catalyst, which was the fall of the Berlin Wall and the death of the Soviet Union. With the onset of a comprehensive default of a large group of countries in the early 90s of the last century, it was necessary to maintain and modernize the existing production for employment and the population's survival.

In this state of shock in all spheres of human life and activity, a new management direction was born: anti-crisis management. A term representing a denial of official rules is nonsense in a linguistic sense but implies a set of urgent actions to survive and mitigate the consequences of a crisis.

At the same time, the massive destruction of both industries and society has led to the need to create a new management system and tools for the survival and maintenance of efficient production facilities before their modernization and technological re-equipment. Working at dozens of enterprises and financial institutions allows me to form a necessary knowledge of impending crisis and prevent bankruptcy.

In contrast to the established procedures, by law, at a time of complete uncertainty and ambiguity in management, the anti-crisis manager takes sole responsibility for carrying out fundamental changes. The National Bankruptcy Law allows him to make any changes, including the possibility of dismissing 100% of staff and selling property in any amount. However, responsibility for the actions of the manager remains for ten years.

Such knowledge and experience formed into the course "Crisis Management Strategies." It quickly began to gain popularity among Online LIGS University students. At the same time, students, being professionals in industries, seeing the attractiveness of the new course, showed a lack of understanding of the latest definitions. How to understand and study this? Did they ask where to find literature?

Unfortunately, there were isolated articles in English and a complete lack of educational literature. Therefore, it was not possible to offer a good set of information for personal research. Even in the United States, it was challenging to find a specialized organization that accumulates statistics and analyzes the crises of individual industries and corporations. One of such organizations is the Crisis management Institute, with active communications conducted. Thus, the experience of crisis analysis and educational methodology, anti-crisis measures for both business and personnel, was borrowed.

Thus, having immature studying basics and a modest literature review is where the reverse conversion chain started our students' research. From the acquired tutor's knowledge and available their industries' examples to forming the concept of anti-crisis measures. Through the building of a business game within the educational program and the objectives joint decision making of the dissertation research. I am very grateful to all the students who carried out unique concepts within the framework of the Crisis Management course and dissertations development. They could drive innovations that, even to me as a professional, were very original and weighty. The high assessment of our students performed on the defense showed scientific and practical value.

As an example of an innovative approach to the development of anti-crisis measures, I will cite several works by our students who have developed models of conversion into the educational process.

Case one. Darrell Wine Fernandez, Doha, Qatar Oil and Gas Corporation ORYX GTL, conducted a unique study of risk and crisis assessment in oilfields within the DBA program.

The industries and companies strive to comply with regulations and anticipate adverse events with constant loss and disaster. One Price of Increased Globalization: More Industrial Accidents

Industrial accidents can be devastating to people and communities. A particular case of the transformation of risks into a corporate, transnational crisis of the last decade is the destruction of the BP drilling platform on April 20, 2010, which led to the death of 11 crew members and many injured.

A management oversight, lack of accountability, ineffective communication, and decision-making — within BP and between contractors

— led to the disaster and over 4.9 million barrels of oil dumped into the Gulf of Mexico.

Case two. Moreover, Ph. D. student Taha Ezzeddin Gorbel has combined operational technology, health, and safety, spending special efforts years of research and educational process to identify communication gaps. He applied classical theories like the Method of Variables and multivariate models to construct an anti-crisis strategy to mitigate the risk of operational management in the oil and gas industry. The developed methodologies integrate well with various sectors and the sphere of social and social sciences.

Taha Ghorbel found that in crises, decision-makers are faced with decisions to take preventive or corrective action. These decisions must be communicated to the participants in the situation, such as the media, public opinion.

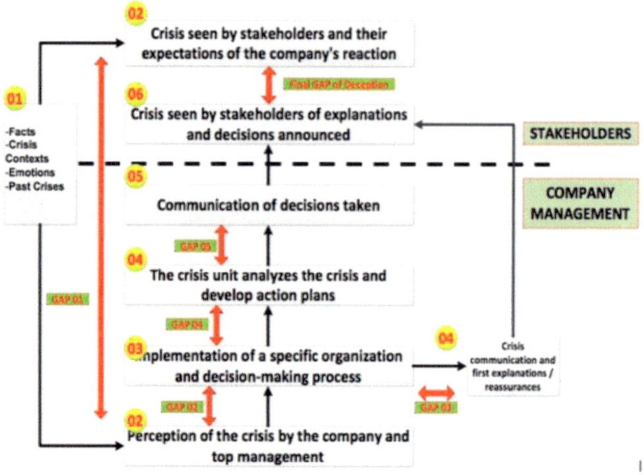

Figure 1.
Stakeholder Dissatisfaction with the Crisis.

Source: Renaudin, H. (2005) Les 5 sources de non qualité de gestion de la crise par l'entreprise.

This diagram (H. Renaudin) explains the five criteria for poor communication. A researcher uses these criteria only to shift perception and communication, shaping a global shift as a crisis. Also, he merged PCA (Principal Component Analysis) method to factorize variables into two primary factors and classify all data into a correlation matrix table. The theory of forecasting strategic actions is quite relevant. This approach can better understand the possible consequences of a crisis and the risk of degeneration after inappropriate decisions, regardless of the sector and the nature of the problem, irrespective of its magnitude, classification based on stakeholder satisfaction that can influence decisions.

This methodology can be a valuable tool for better-assisting policymakers in times of crisis.

Case three. I mainly want to note striking and many studied examples of how formed Singapore's strategies within the industry 4.0 and 5.0 trends framework. Dr. Tan Kian Hua, Singapore, co-author of these theses and an expert in cybersecurity, cloud technologies, and the Internet of Things for the social and industrial sphere, as a student, was able to research and defend a thesis in a short time during such rapid changes in information and communication systems. Both in his research and his professional life, he is actively involved in the cybersecurity field. For example, he participates in Singapore's "Smart Nation and Smart City" program, which can technically be presented as a large-scale set of devices that can communicate with each other and are easy to manage. Such phenomena as hacking and phishing and other destructive mechanisms for modern databases and cloud technologies.

The region's countries have no aspirations to challenge Singapore's leadership in structural innovation; it is open to severe horizontal integration and shares transformation through joint ventures and international "Hi-Tech" cooperation. Most of Russia's regional and corporate leaders, for example, have visited, got acquainted, and understood the scale of the "smart nation" strategy.

Case four. Within such scaling and cross-industrial cooperative science, former student and now the University Tutor Dr. Nguyen Ming made unique research "ENHANCING SATELLITE COMMUNICATION BANDWIDTH EFFICIENCY, AND COST SAVINGS THROUGH TECHNOLOGICAL INNOVATION AND MANAGEMENT PROCESS" with his study deeply entered the spacecraft management to improve their performance.

Case five. And student Kenneth A. Shay seminar paper "AN INDISPENSABLE REQUISITE FOR MICRO, SMALL AND MEDIUM ENTERPRISES AND NGOs IN JAMAICA" is considering Anti-crisis management within world globalization consequences. Being an expert in NGOs, NCOs he was involved in many countries in the Caribbean region disasters' and understood how it dipper depending on the small and medium businesses surviving. Also, he had perfectly decomposed the anti-crisis measures synergy to resolve social crises of island states after typhoons and floods.

Case six. LIGS University students have efficiently integrated the research methodology into the transformation of international business when creating joint ventures affecting the development of local industries, MS business. The accompanying and political influence of political crises. A unique example is the scientific work of Dr. Youssouf Doukoure, France, associated with the development of international telecommunications in the context of cooperation between economies in transition and developed countries.

All this was accompanied by incredible innovative reflections and our researchers who, in the absence of a good literature review and awareness of events, can develop the necessary measures to ensure the safety and performance of subjects and technologies.

Moreover, the ongoing partnership of students with their supervisor leads to joint work on improving educational methodologies, writing articles, and publishing books. The best example is the partnership with Tan Kian Hua and Taha Ghorbel. As well as distributing skills on the international level.

Case seven. Moreover, the principles of the professor-students cooperation for researching and this designing expand on an international scale. But I will also give a vivid example of a young transformation, the initiative of two Russian master students of the SHFM, RANEPA 2019, Vasilisa Usoltseva and Ksenia Kovaleva, whose leader I had the honor to be. They did good research and defended their dissertation with excellent marks on the topic: COURSE FOR FINTECH: MARKET DEVELOPMENT IN THE RUSSIAN FEDERATION ON THE EXAMPLE OF THE REPUBLIC OF SINGAPORE. A simple but not isolated example of a generation of people coming to the industry can think globally and act locally.

Case eight. The decline in the quality of educational programs is becoming evident. For traditional universities that find themselves in a crisis of communications, as an example of my work within the Russian Academy of National Economic and Public Service and at the Belarusian State Economic University, where I conduct English-language programs for international students. Especially education, students of traditional universities and postgraduate education programs are today asking about the adequacy of the knowledge gained and the costs invested in their education. Transformations from the offline classical education system are hybrid, and online education for non-specialized universities turned out to be very painful and flawed, which is possible.

Of course, conducting online seminars for groups of students of 20-30 or more people is challenging and ineffective. At the same time, the advantages of a system of online universities with a technologically established system of personal support for each student are apparent. Such a model of the future one-to-one education is inevitably accompanied by a

considerable number of communication systems and the implementation of research projects.
And that will give new tools for the formation. The synergy mechanisms will

convert economic, financial, social, and political knowledge into a new post- industrial professional and ethical code. The digital world should be used simultaneously. Today our students undertake to research the effectiveness of such projects on an international scale.

Case nine. Modern students, in their research, go much further and explore the crises of recent years, such as COVID and the technological explosion that led to the system of online communications, which also undoubtedly influenced the educational process.

Today our students undertake to research the effectiveness of such projects on an international scale. I will give just a couple of such examples of students from Canada. Elias Enoaku with research title: Investigation of the causes of megaprojects crisis of international development cooperation and sustainability projects leading to failures: Based on trends and triggers of project failures in Sub Saharan Africa and Cameroon as a case study. Adinet Lock will consider Crisis management in British Columbia: A strategy for recovery within the reasons and people behavior during the COVID and beyond.

Case ten. The history of the transformation of knowledge into skills experience in various fields and between generations shows that each development level and technology requires separate mechanisms for the conversion and adaptation of the IT and Image methodologies used.

Students of the first generations of secondary schools had a significant difference in their knowledge in studies. There was always a problem of transformation through generations. However, in the modern digital world, when a child, long before pronouncing the first words, can easily find a way to turn on the desired program on a smartphone, this is especially noticeable. It is not surprising that Generation Y and Z, who grew up in the rapidly evolving ecosystem involving the Internet and social networks, can interact with the virtual world and influence behavior and thinking.

Now the question is acute when we should make significant concessions to the younger generation. Should we shift responsibility to their self-government at such a young age? Nevertheless, we have to assume that they will soon be employers, including for the older generations, for whom traditional employment is rapidly disappearing.

Case eleven. In the practical transformation example, I want to highlight the experience of Finland, which, 40 years ago, was considered a country of woodworking and with a developing industrial potential, agriculture, and forestry engineering. Today this country, modest and close to our mentality, is a recognized European leader in information technologies, both an integrator and a developer. Yet, without ambitions for the status of "smart nation," Finland is confidently following the path of "Smart Industry," abandoning hydrocarbons in the energy and industrial sectors, satisfying the needs of renewable sources, except nuclear energy.

Enterprises and urban infrastructures are tuned for nature-like technologies, digitalization, and safe and comfortable living "Human being." A concrete example of such a peaceful Finnish industrial revolution can be convincingly shown by my partners of the Consulting Group "SPROF" specializing in the problems of operational productivity and efficiency of enterprises and organizations. By pursuing business excellence armed with motivation for staff and commitment to new essential skills, they convince clients: "All businesses are undergoing significant change. Even on the brink of hype, digitalization initiatives are critical and therefore cannot be belittled in any way, as they can depend on the survival of a business. But even digitalization requires change management; the new software is only part of the solution. You need first to define the strategic designs, structure, and business processes of your enterprise."

Thus, two questions arise: first, how exactly can you locate your plant in the industry and estimate how much money your business is currently losing or will require in the future? Second, are these losses mainly due to lack of governance, process disruption, lack of competence, or a desire to keep up with the leader? Does an additional question arise for each of us? Is it worth everyone to strive for a bright post-industrial future?

The past decades have been replete with global connections in technologies and processes that have transformed multinational companies. Let me give you a familiar story. In the 1980s and 1990s, Lean Manufacturing was a Big New Idea, and it seemed like everyone was learning new instruments with Japanese names. But too many companies' efforts to "get lean" have settled on tools to help people become more efficient. Even today, research confirms that only 26% of major organizational transformations are successful.

So when leaders think about their organization's digital priorities - its digital strategy - they need to identify the technologies and applications that would have the most significant potential impact. Finally, we must remember that technology alone is not a panacea. Instead, it is the people who apply this technology in their daily work that create added value.

The digital transformation worked for countries and organizations because their leaders went back to basics: they focused on changing the mindset of their members and organizational culture and processes before they decided which digital tools and how to use them. As a result, what participants see for the organization's future has driven technology, not the other way around? Therefore, with the synergy of Singaporean and Finnish thinking, we acquired international competencies, try to transform future skills into a cross-cultural professional environment flexibly and the structure of transitional economies of our countries.

Summary and conclusion

The life cycle of a person is equal to the period of education.

Studying at foreign universities and working in international organizations, especially teaching experience on different continents, have created an invaluable resource. As a result, the entire postgraduate education system in developed countries builds on very high requirements and a conscientious attitude towards learning.

Students' interest and desire for independent knowledge and scientific research give us a great incentive to cooperate and achieve the best results in education and preparation for a dissertation. In addition, we can use information technology and give students an assessment as honestly as possible by combining traditional, online, and mixed teaching methods.

Despite many trained leaders at all levels of government and communication, the lack of real progress, many nations are worried about the question, "What went wrong?" The current generation needs to develop a new management system to replace the traditional one, introduce new models of interaction and cooperation that allow doing twenty steps in one direction, not one step in 20ty directions. We are beginning to understand the new beyond COVID norm, which will be in force until the end of the year, possibly in the foreseeable future. A flexible study and work environment for education or multimodal courses combining online and full-time students is by far the most common learning scenario—critical words in this concept: flexibility and maneuverability.

These issues will have to be addressed by the current and future generations of both the National and the World communities inhabiting our space called the Humanity and Artificial Intelligence Union.

Afterword

This article was prepared for a long time, with inspiration to give the local and international community, in which I, as one of the authors, led, studying, living, and working in joy for fifty years, our analysis of both current events and historical trends in the field of education. Everything stated positively; the practicality of such an opinion was carefully considered and repeatedly thought out using a literary review. We will be grateful for feedback and suggestions, preserving our cooperation and contributing to successful development.

Contact information

Dr.VladimirBiruk, Professor of LIGS University, Capital Group Director; www.capital.by bvg1952@gmail.com +375 29 1280478

Dr. Tan KianHua, Singapore, Gen. Director of Information Security Accorix Pte Ltd, Smart Nation Smart City Program. kian_hua_tan@hotmail.com

Ph.D. Taha Ezzeddin Gorbel; QHSE Management Expert, Eni Corporate University - QHSE Training Coordinator Eni Development Project in Iraq; +9647809261320, ghorbeltaha@gmail.com

DBA. Darrell Wine Fernandez, Doha, Qatar Oil and Gas Corporation ORYX GTL, Chief Technical Assistant - Business Development. fdaryl@hotmail.com

Dr. Youssouf Doukoure, France, Director of Bincady Security co-ny, Versaille Academy. Tel. 0033618941911 drdoukoure.youssouf@gmail.com

Kim Karma, Finland, CMC, General Director and Partner of SPROF Group kim@karme.fi kim.karme@cmc-global.org

Nikita Shanovich, The Institute of education Development CAPITAL, Ernst&Yong, Senior Expert shanovich.nikita@gmail.com

How Technological Changes Affect the Human Behavior

Adedayo Adetayo

Abstract

Technology is diverse; however, individual exposure to technology impacts how one behaves. Its advancement has been perfected to the extent that most technological gadgets rely on things such as touchscreen for operations. The impact of this has been researched, and it leads back to the effect that individuals feel due to interactions with a screen. A systematic literature review was done to complete the research, and the data gathered is both qualitative and quantitative. Essential takeaways point that technology impacts opinions and attention that people give to details; brain elasticity is related to digital media. Extended use of technology impacts mental health, and the eventual outcome is the attitude to life and health. Which, in positive environments, bring about an elevated feel to the person using it. Since exposure to technology is sure to happen, the author concludes that coming into contact with technology will rewire the brain, impact moods, improve the way we receive and provide information and change the general direction of life.

Keywords: Technology, mental impact, Behavior

JEL Classification: O- Economic Development, Innovation, Technological Change and Growth, M- Business Administration, J- Labour and Demographic Economics

Introduction

Technology advancements take the upper hand in our lives; humans have grown dependent on it for simple tasks and continuous providence of information. The mobile phone has taken the upper hand; commands such as "Hey Siri" and "hey google" are common when individuals seek to find something from their phones. It is thus evident that we are significantly dependent on technology. As technology is further refined, our dependency on it increases. The evolution of intelligent devices, artificial intelligence and the modern workplace all result from technology. The reliance on technology is quite high that business processes revolve around it. Automation, e- commerce, social media, and e-learning all show the extent to which individual and commercial operations are penned on technology (Cascio & Montealegre, 2016. Pp. 349). Our memories are even embedded in technological devices. Raising the question, to what extent are humans dependent on technology? Have there been changes in behaviours due to overreliance on technology? By exploring the various aspects of technology use, a conclusion is reached on how it affects human behaviours.

A Table Showing the Integration Of Technology In Society

Figure 1. ***The History of Computing and its Integration into Society***

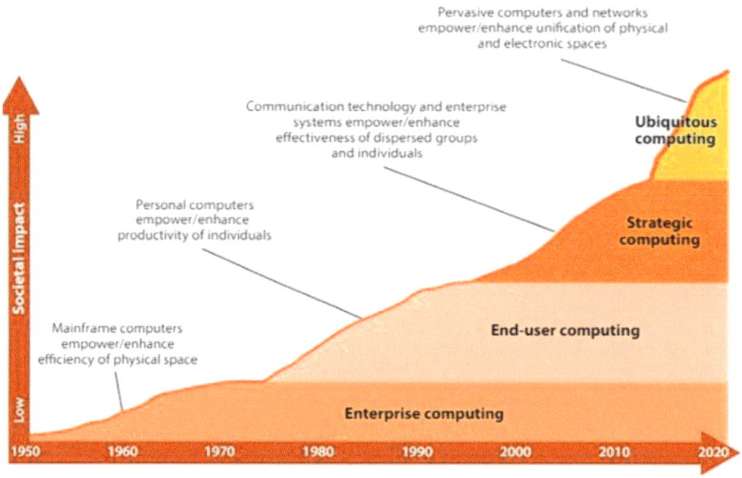

Source: Cascio & Montealegre, 2016, pp. 352

Data and Methodology

Methodology

To get information on how technology impacts human behaviours, a systematic literature review will be done to filter information. The study seeks to answer the question, how does technology change impact human behaviours? The approach to complete the review entails using reproducible methods to select and critically appraise relevant research. The approach is ideal as it answers a focused research question, employs a reproducible research strategy, assesses all results for inclusion or exclusion and offers a biased summary of findings.

Data

Secondary data is to be used. The systematic quantitative review will be used for the research. Focus is on studies that have numerical data due to comparison ease and replicability. Qualitative data is used to expound on information gathered. Moreover, secondary data offers a timeline, thus ease in comparison and information derivation.

Results and Discussion

Impact on Opinions and Attention to Details

Mandellos, Tsipianitis and Lymberopoulos, (2019) closely examined the impact technology has on individual opinions. More so, how open people are to new information and the extent to which they reveal knowledge. A study conducted on students required them to reveal how they feel about studies, particular lessons, and laboratory sessions. People's opinion is likely to change with the scenario that individuals are exposed to. There is also a possibility that less attention is given to individual tasks when completed via technology as compared to when they are done manually. From the work of Mandellos et al. 2019, Pp. 501), it is evident that the level of honesty differs among general questions, teacher-specific, lesson-specific and questions examining students' level of responsibility. It is also evident that through technology, individual opinions and behaviours significantly change compared to when no technology is used. For instance, the fear of technology revealing personal identity coerces most to change opinion. Moreover, technology lowers individual attention levels. It corrects errors and reminds them of the task; this is unlike the traditional approach where papers call for utmost attention as little room is available for changes.

A Table Comparing the Use Of Digital And Hardcopy Forms In Class

Figure 2. ***Comparing the Filling Rate of Hardcopy and Softcopy Questionnaires***

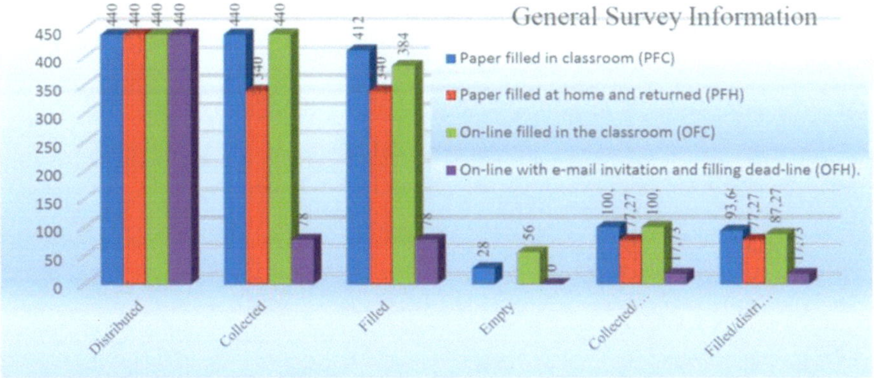

Source: Mandellos et al., 2019.

From the table, it is evident that hardcopy papers are easily filled compared to softcopies as people rely on technology to remind them.

Impact on Mental Health

Mental health is a significant indicator of human behaviours. When coupled with technology, more revelation is brought to light on the individual's condition. Moreover, evidence shows that technology gradually changes an individual's ways of thinking and mannerism. Bahman and Farhang, (2019, Pp. 355) examine the different ways through which technology impacts mental health. They note that communication bombards us with information affecting our mental health and making it hard to adjust. Currently, everyone is exposed to large volumes of data and, consequently, a significant volume of information. People are differently exposed to information. As per the American psychological association, people are more likely to use different mediums, with teenagers preferring Instagram and Snapchat. The primary challenge with this has been the creation of the constant checker. As of 2019, more than 43% of the United States population comprises constant checkers (Bahman and Farhang, 2019, PP. 357). The result is that continuous checkers are more exposed to mental health issues as compared to non-checkers.

There is evidence to show that the habits arising from the prolonged use of social media impact the users.

More so, practices such as the desire to remain digitally connected, deriving happiness from social media, and feelings of isolation when cut off from social channels are rampant among individuals addicted to social media checkers (Bahman and Farhang, 2019). In the long run, issues such as depression arise, taking individuals deeper into the rabbit hole. On children, they lack the connections that arise with family and grow aggressive over time due to massive exposure to violent video games.

A Figure Illustrating The Impact Of Different Social Channels On Individuals

Figure 3. ***The Net Impact of Social Media on the Mental Health of Individuals***

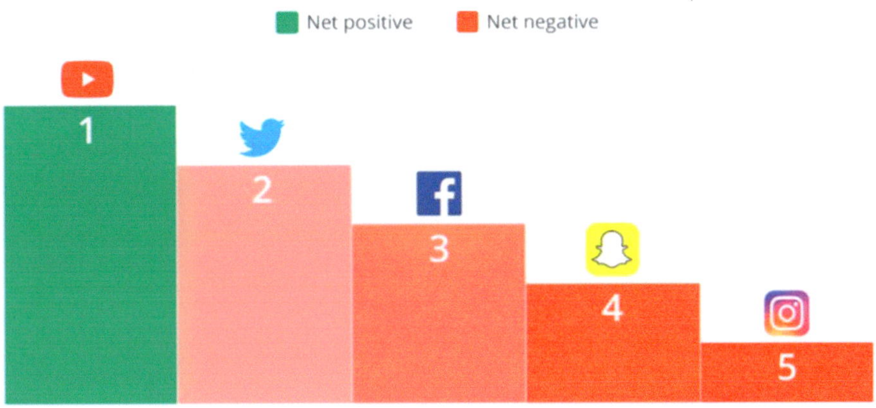

Source: RSPH, 2021

From the table, it is evident that social sites that allow people to learn about others heavily impact individuals' mental well-being. Site with less personal interactions has little impact on individuals.

Brain Elasticity Related to Digital Media

A simple way to examine if digital media impacts the human brain is by examining the impact of touchscreens on human actions. The test is through determining changes that have occurred to the somatosensory cortex part of the brain. There is evidence to show that the cortical space is used for tactile receptors on the fingertips, and it is influenced by hand use. For instance, string players have a significant number of cortical neurons of the somatosensory cortex assigned to the fingers playing the instruments. The scenario is also evidenced in repeated grasp movement, such as the use of touchscreens gadgets. From the work of Korte (2020, Pp. 105), there is evidence that repeated use of touchscreens impacts the somatosensory cortex. The long-term impact is that the development may occur at the expense of other motor coordination skills. The development or delay in motor skills is correlated with screen time; therefore, the cortical space development comes at the expense of motor skills due to an overall lack of exercise.

While the development of motor skills may delay, there is evidence to show that other aspects of brain development may be hastened (Korte, 2020, Pp. 108). Language, cognition and perception are enhanced through technology. Aspects such as semantics and grammar heavily rely on how information is presented. Through digital media, the information presented is enhanced and positively influences comprehension (Korte, 2020, Pp. 108). Reading habits may also change through electronic media, with a higher inclination in a positive direction. On the ageing brain, digital sources have proven to increase the attention span and an elevated cognition level among the elderly (Hoehe & Thibaut, 2020).

Attitude Towards Life and Health

Mejova and Kalimeri (2019) provide the lead on the impact technology has on the desire to remain fit. Attention is paid to how individuals receive and incorporate information for their daily use. Currently, technology is highly used in the war against obesity. Pushing for the adoption of health and fitness applications. There is evidence to show that individuals who adopt technology use generally have a positive attitude to life in their daily use. For instance, they pay attention to particular activities. Applications with more users are highly marketed as ideal for tracking certain activities like walking or running (Cascio and Montealegre, 2016). There is the creation of socioeconomic status with individuals who exercise regularly perceiving themselves of higher socioeconomic status. The discussion of values and happiness are incorporated into everyday life; this arises due to a regular schedule that helps create the illusion of achievements. There is the possibility of focusing more on positive behaviours such as walking and exercising more when technology is used than when none of it is applied.

Discussion

The general approach towards life is greatly influenced by technology. There is a relation between the brain and how people live based on technology, with a more significant incline towards individuals heavily relying on technology for survival. Moreover, the development patterns of the brain depend on the extent of technology use. There is a direct impact on an opinion that people hold when technology is in use from the research. Furthermore, the effect on mental health and brain elasticity related to brain activity is also evident. The long-term impact is a complete change in the attitude that people hold towards life. The four impacts of technology are directly related. As one continuously uses technology, their brains will change, perfecting the use of technological devices, brains become more receptive to information, and outwardly, individuals are much happier due to perception of class and feel of satisfaction based on accomplishments.

Conclusion

Human behaviours are sure to change with the use of technology. However, the technology that one has access to and its use determines the direction that individual behaviours will take. Issues such as brain development, attitudes and moods that individuals have relied on the technology they are exposed to. In a nutshell, exposure to technology rewires the brain, impacts moods, enhances the reception and provision of information and creates new ways of life.

References

1. Bahman, Z., & Farhang, M. (2019). The Impact of Technology on Human Behavior. A Model To Forecast Future Paradigms, 403-416. https://doi.org/ 10.1201/9781003000662-9

2. Cascio, W., & Montealegre, R. (2016). How Technology Is Changing Work and Organizations. Annual Review Of Organizational Psychology And Organizational Behavior, 3(1), 349-375. https://doi.org/10.1146/annurev-orgpsych-041015-062352

3. Hoehe, M., & Thibaut, F. (2020). Going digital: how technology use may influence human brains and behavior. Dialogues In Clinical Neuroscience,

22(2), 93-97. https://doi.org/10.31887/dcns.2020.22.2/mhoehe

4. Korte, M. (2020). The impact of the digital revolution on human brain and behavior: where do we stand?. Dialogues In Clinical Neuroscience, 22(2), 101-111. https://doi.org/10.31887/dcns.2020.22.2/mkorte

5. Mandellos, G., Tsipianitis, D., & Lymberopoulos, D. (2019). Can information technology affects people's behavior and opinion? A way to identify it. IFAC-Papersonline, 52(25), 498-503. https://doi.org/10.1016/j.ifacol.2019.12.593

6. Mejova, Y., & Kalimeri, K. (2019). Effect of Values and Technology Use on Exercise. Proceedings Of The 27Th ACM Conference On User Modeling, Adaptation And Personalization. https://doi.org/10.1145/3320435.3320451

7. RSPH. (2021). Royal Society for Public Health UK. Rsph.org.uk. Retrieved 17 May 2021, from https://www.rsph.org.uk/.

8. Sullivan, A., & Lachman, M. (2017). Behavior Change with Fitness Technology in Sedentary Adults: A Review of the Evidence for Increasing Physical Activity. Frontiers In Public Health, 4. https://doi.org/10.3389/fpubh.2016.00289

Contact information

Name of the author: Adedayo Adetayo
Affiliation (University): Horizon University
Email: adedayo.adetayo0708@huparis.eu

How Technological Changes Affect the Human Behavior

Nnenna Uboma

Abstract

Technological changes are one of the major concerns in a developing world and their impact on human behavior. Due to social distancing norms and nationwide lockdowns, the Covid-19 pandemic has inevitably resulted in an increase in the use of digital technology. People and organizations around the world have had to adapt to new jobs and lifestyles. As a result of increased digitalization, more businesses and educational institutions are adopting work-from-home policies. Blockchain technology has become increasingly relevant, necessitating design and regulatory analysis. The number of gig workers and the gig economy is growing, raising concerns about job distribution, teamwork, motivation, and work overload and presenteeism (Pandey, & Pal, 2020, pp.4-14). With an increase in digital presence, workplace surveillance and technostress problems will become more prevalent. Online fraud is likely to increase, as is research into security management. This research aims at scrutinizing how all these possible repercussions of technological changes influence how humans behave as they continuously interact with the systems involved.

Keywords: Behavior change, Technology and Covid-19, Technology on behavior

JEL Classification: O33, I12, M310

Introduction

Technology is the combination of techniques, knowledge, processes and methods used to produce goods and services. Technology changes mean the alteration of ways of doing things based on the existing conditions. The Covid- 19 is one of the issues that illustrated how the world could establish and adopt the change to force people to accept new ideas. In the 2010s, various transformations in technology and the underlying impacts on people's lives were a key part of social development compared to the past years. This paper aims at determining technology developments are proportional to human behavior either in the negative and positive. It is meant to adopt some insights from the Covid-19 pandemic where people changed their ways of life especially considering the need to establish social distance and increased reduction in interpersonal contacts.

Research Problem

Technology changes are an area receiving much interest in the world today. Mixed reactions have been emerging based on the influence that various technologies bring in society. These changes have been criticized on the different social evils they present in the world with children and youths being the major impacted groups in various circumstances. However, various circumstances force people to embrace the various changes in technology because of the facilitation provided in handling different roles in society. This was witnessed when Covid-19 struck the world, requiring people to work from home. Technology was embraced when people realized that Covid-19 was a public issue that would last longer than expected (Elson, & Przybylski, 2017, pp.4-6). This paper is based on the contemplation that societal behaviors are prone to change based on the emerging issues in technology and how it requires one to adhere to the provided guidelines.

Research Questions

1. What are the different impacts those technological changes likely to establish on people?
2. Do technological changes impact people's culture, and to what extent?
3. How did technological changes affect workplace behavior during the Covid-19 pandemic?

Research Objectives

To measure how technology is beneficial for society during pandemics.

To determine how people behaviors are impacted when changes in technology call for lifestyle alterations.

To determine how technology can create an enabling environment for remote working.
To learn the changes in people and impression in technology when Covid-19 struck the world

Background Study

Technological transformation is reported to establish a proportional transformation of people's behaviors in any society. Although there is usually a rebellious spirit that sometimes forces people to remain reluctant to the transformation, there usually comes when most of them accept it. In most cases, much rebellion originates from propaganda and misconception when there are indicated repercussions of how immoral society would become. Nevertheless, technology has been changing over the years, with every decade experiencing some transformation. For instance, technology has been witnessed from the simple gadgets used such as smartphones, laptops, iPhones, smartwatches, artificial intelligence and other practices connected to effectiveness in working and interaction (Hilty, & Chan, 2018, p.52). Amazingly, some people may criticize technology, but it is sometimes unknowingly at the heart of their lives.

One of the major transformations through technological changes is communication. It appears that people have completely changed the ways they connect with others either in families, businesses and any of the social interaction agenda. The use of the internet has increased connection among people, whereby the online platform has enhanced the exchange of information and ideas. This has been witnessed even more during the emergence of Covid-19, where people were required to work remotely to avoid interpersonal contacts. The use of technological gadgets such as laptops and smartphones has been one of the major attributes that has indicated the importance of technological changes.

When Covid-19 struck, people were forced to invest more in technology to ensure that they continue with their usual activities when the pandemic inhibited one-on-one working almost everywhere in the world. Besides working, work training and recruitment required that people adopt the available online alternatives to ensure they avoid close interactions as much as possible (Barnes, 2020, p.107). The education sector was also not left behind in this practice where video-conferencing software was used to connect students with instructors. This struck the world more than what society could contemplate in the recent years before a pandemic that could limit one-on-one interactions emerged.

Considering the previous years before Covid-19, there were about 40% internet users in the world. This then rose abruptly to almost 100% when people had no alternative but to adhere to the protocols set for the pandemic (Yan, Gaspar, & Zhu, 2021, p.5). More seriousness across countries emerged when the cessation of movement and lockdown associated with the pandemic emerged. Information systems and networks surged in use and became the norm for most people in the majorly impacted regions.

Another major area that witnessed a change in human behavior was the acceptance of digital money. Even people who were very committed to cash transfers have been forced to appreciate payments and recipients through digital transactions either because the transacting parties are far apart or the liquid money exchange would impose more infections for the virus. This has also been a major transformation in the financial sector, where institutions are forced to adjust their practices to accommodate Covid-19 guidelines that would enable them to remain in business (Hilty, & Chan, 2018, pp.55-56). Similar issues have been witnessed across other businesses where interactions between the buyers and sellers become virtualized. This has been a behavior-transforming aspect across all social groups, including the young and the elderly. Indeed, there was an immense transformation of the traditional cash exchanges to adopt the more effective practices when remote processes take the best part of the society.

Again, privacy has become a major part of behavior transformation associated with technological changes. As people deploy virtual operations using technology, there is always a choice on how they are willing to share information and other important ideas. This has also promoted limited selection for the level of connections across any individual

(Narayanamurthy, & Tortorella, 2021, 109-110). It also means that the traditional office behaviors are not further impacting employees. This has therefore facilitated to alleviate the possible repercussions originating from poor interactions among the different groups. Amidst the privacy is the ease of connection across individuals because of the reduced movements. With the ability of technology to perform many operations than in the traditional social and working environments, distance connections are facilitated.

Materials and Methods

Materials

1. Questionnaire for online survey
2. Ms Excel package for data analysis

Methods

Mixed studies using both quantitative and qualitative methods were used in data collection and analysis. An online survey using a questionnaire with both close-ended and open-ended questions was used. The close-ended section was meant to collect quantitative data, while the open-ended was effective for qualitative data (Gibson, 2017, p.154). The methods were necessary to develop the various themes from primary data based on how the scrutinized respondents indicated their personal experiences. To undertake this, 100 participants were selected, of whom 60 were males and 40 females between the age of 18 and 75 years old. The themes developed through the qualitative data were then further expanded quantitatively. These categories of participants were engaged because they are categorized as having a better understanding of technology use and the impacts they felt.

To collect data, a random sampling technique was used to choose participants. This alleviated biases that could be established as a result of selectivity. Random sampling provided an equal probability for all the subjects to be engaged in the study. This was from the understanding that Covid-19 impacted everyone in the world (Etikan, & Bala, 2017, p.64). For this survey, respondents from Canada were considered to establish measurable data. The survey was distributed to the participants through emails they provided upon request after interacting through social media. Facebook, Instagram and Twitter were the basic communication platforms that offered an appropriate podium to connect with respondents.

Results and Discussions

Results

The study used 100 respondents in the initial request for participation. However, only 95 of the delivered surveys were successively responded to. These 95 respondents were considered for the results and analysis.

Table 1. ***Results of the Study***

Impact on behavior (Theme)	Responses	
	Yes	No
Better communication efficiency	63	32
Appreciated digital money transactions	76	19
Better privacy	48	47
Reduced work stress	66	29
Improved family relationships	58	37
Better connection to the world	75	20
Improved social relations	47	48
Reduced cultural connection	73	22
Changed spending behaviors	58	37
Improved problem-solving behavior	40	55

Source: the Author

Table 2. ***Results of the Study***

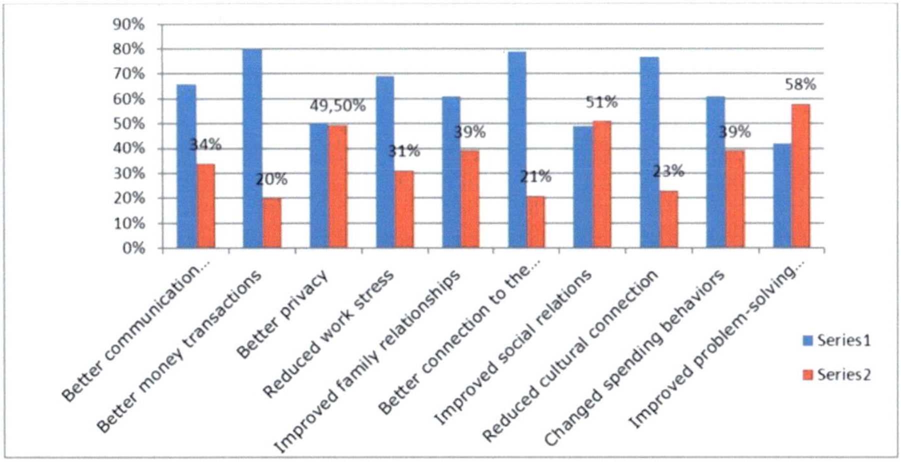

Source: Human Behavior and Emerging Technologies, 3(1), 5.

Discussion

The illustrated data and themes illustrated in the Table 2 above were generated from the insights acquired from the online survey. These themes were developed to understand better the different concepts respondents provided across the research.

Better Communication Efficiency

Communication efficiency was a measure of how well the society would connect more, better and faster through the technological changes during Covid-19. Most organizations providing virtual communication services were witnessed to improve their levels of services to allow more users through their systems. In this, 66% of the respondents scrutinized agreed with this aspect. As the movement of people across different regions was avoided, people could be able to better connect with others remotely. There was a high probability of getting in touch even with people not able to connect previously as one-on-one interaction is usually limited to time and distance. However, technological changes and more orientation to telecommunication offered an adequate opportunity to communicate. People are likely to maintain this practice even in future.

Better Digital Money Transactions

Money transactions are a common practice that defines daily societal behaviors. It is rare for anyone, especially in adulthood, to evade such transactions, especially when making purchases. This was one of the major areas that experienced a change in human behavior through technological changes. The Covid-19 pandemic increased this phenomenon as people were warned from using liquid cash because of the high probability to cause Covid-19 infections. People then developed a norm to use digital money transfers even when purchasing consumer products. In this study, 80% accepted that technology changes in this sector was helpful and reduced most constraints witnessed earlier, such as having to wait for balances. Some even commented that this was attractive because of how it also enhanced hygiene.

Better Privacy

Privacy issues are what society is always cognizant about. People are usually obliged to safeguarding personal data, which they believe that limited accessibility should occur. Technological changes had an impact on how people perceived their privacy. In this, respondents had mixed reactions on how working digitally safeguarded them or put them at risk. This had 50.5% of the respondents accepting better security as they could preserve their data as they worked remotely. They believed that they developed personalized behaviors which were not present at the workplace where employees and other stakeholders could easily access data. However, the major concern with the other respondents was cyber insecurity claiming that there was a high probability of cybercrime because of excessive internet use.

Reduced Work Stress

Stress in the workplace is a common phenomenon, especially when one has to work under strict supervision. From the study, 69% of the respondents indicated that they were comfortable working online because of the opportunity. One can easily relax and continue with the tasks later. One of the major impacts of this aspect was improved productivity as one could easily select the best period when one can perform extremely well. In most cases, the workplace environment can cause fatigue and reduced productivity. However, the digital transformation created an opportunity to establish a healthy lifestyle where one can maximize the most productive period. This was relatively essential and allowed individuals to change the various schedules based on how they believed would reduce stress. They would also balance between work and home activities.

Improved Family Relationships

Family relationship was another important theme considered in the wake of technological changes. Before Covid-19, there were many cases where families highly disintegrated because of the tight working schedules. However, technology use, especially through digital platforms, was emphasized. In this, 61% indicated to have improved family relationships considering that they were able to work from home and, as a result, interact with each other. There were even comments that they could make better and collective decisions that would rather take longer or never occur in their lifetimes. As a result, people could pay much attention to their loved ones, which was not always possible when the pandemic was absent in Canada and the world.

Better Connection to the World

One of the greatest perceptions of human behavior impact through technological developments is the connection and understanding of the world. For this, 79% of the respondents acknowledged having a better opportunity to comprehend better what takes place in various global issues. The interest in how other parts of the world was fairing during the pandemic was one of the key interests. Indeed, many people remained glued to their gadgets to better understand even some issues such as politics. Therefore, people had to change how they appreciate or provoke diversity, considering that technology provides such opportunities. As some activities such as moving across the globe are usually limited to the various constraints, it is only through technology that people can learn a lot. It is also from technology changes that cultural integration has been facilitated by selecting the positive behaviors and suppressing those that seem misleading.

Improved Social Relations

Social relations usually develop when people can connect with others across different platforms. This issue received mixed reactions from the respondents such that they are almost balanced in accepting and rejecting the perception. Out of those surveyed, only 49% agreed with the concept that technological changes increase social relations. Most of the respondents believed that one-on-one relationships are the key to build strong and sustainable relations. Considering the Covid-19 pandemic, most people part ways and promoted an individualist culture where people were to remain by themselves with limited interactions with others. As such, some relations require platforms that would allow physical connections, which technology cannot offer. People are misled to believe that there is no much connection required by just chatting with others online. This has also been indicated as one of the major causes of social evils just because people have not learned enough of how to deal with social relationships and how to deal with conflicts when they occur.

Reduced Cultural Connection

People's cultures and practices seem to be greatly impacted by technological changes. They usually claim to modernity and consider their norms obsolete.

This is relatively evident when people rely much on technology. Cultural activities usually progress when communities can come together and perform particular customs that align with their orientations. In this case, 77% of those surveyed accepted that technology has been impacting and reducing how they attach to their cultures and activities. The situation escalated even more during Covid-19, when people were forced to avoid movements that could impose infections. This challenge increases even more across generations, with those younger having greater problems in handling cultural issues.

Changed Spending Behavior

Spending is an issue which everyone is willing to establish ways to govern. Technology changes have come with diverse impacts, some of which may reduce spending or retain it at the actual position. In this, 61% accepted the changed spending in various aspects with most indicating on reduction. For instance, the expenses required to move from one place to the other are eliminated by working digitally and achieving even more. Organizations have also been able to establish an adequate operations platform that provides a proper work environment. This is also connected to process automation, sometimes requiring lower human resource to handle tasks, thereby reducing labor cost. People have adopted the culture of accepting to avoid physical activity as the paramount aspect to handle tasks and operations. Becoming systematic has also been a key aspect in reducing the efforts required to handle various tasks effectively and promptly.

Improved Problemsolving

The world is full of issues that usually demand techniques that would support a problem-solving culture. Technology advancements are some of the areas humans have invested in to establish better and faster techniques to use in solving the different issues in their lives. Despite the positive impact technology has imposed during Covid-19, only 42% accepted that it effectively solved problem-solving. One of the major reasons for disagreement included the aspect that many conflicts in families have been witnessed during the pandemic, and hence a major gap established requiring a better approach. This indicates that the technology could be effective in the working platforms but has great deficiencies across family relations.

Conclusion

Technology has been one of the major aspects in transforming human behavior, especially during Covid-19. As the study illustrates, people and organizations have been able to do more despite the challenges. It was identified that behavior change occurred in both positive and negative aspects based on the underlying impacts and the more favored side. One of the major areas considered was social constructs, including relationships, cultural connections and family issues. These are always core to consider because they are relatively instrumental. The major area of importance in technological change in transforming human behavior was the workplace. This section of society was considered relatively in need of advancements in the methods of undertaking different operations. Speed, efficiency and accuracy were identified as essential in technology change. Generally, society has embraced technological changes from providing an enabling environment in functions and output, especially during Covid-19.

References

1. Barnes, S. J. (2020). Information management research and practice in the post-COVID-19 world. International Journal of Information Management, 55, 102175.
2. Elson, M., & Przybylski, A. K. (2017). The science of technology and human behavior.
3. Etikan, I., & Bala, K. (2017). Sampling and sampling methods. Biometrics & Biostatistics International Journal, 5(6), 00149.
4. Hilty, D. M., & Chan, S. (2018). Human behavior with mobile health: smartphone/devices, apps and cognition. Psychol Cogn Sci, 4(2), 36-47.
5. Gibson, C. B. (2017). Elaboration, generalization, triangulation, and interpretation: On enhancing the value of mixed method research. Organizational Research Methods, 20(2), 193-223.

6. Narayanamurthy, G., & Tortorella, G. (2021). Impact of COVID-19 outbreak on employee performance–moderating role of industry 4.0 base technologies. International Journal of Production Economics, 234, 108075.
7. Pandey, N., & Pal, A. (2020). Impact of digital surge during Covid-19

pandemic: A viewpoint on research and practice. International Journal of Information Management, 55, 102171.
8. Yan, Z., Gaspar, R., & Zhu, T. (2021). How humans behave with emerging technologies during the COVID-19 pandemic?. Human Behavior and Emerging Technologies, 3(1), 5.

Contact information

Name of the author: Nnenna Uboma

Affiliation (University): TD Bank Senior Manager, Risk Analytics

Email: nnenna.uboma@yahoo.ca

How Technological Changes Affect the Human Behavior

Laura A. McCoy

Abstract

With the development of Digital Data, we live in a time when we can communicate directly with individual customers. We can reach parts of the world as business owners that were isolated during previous decades. We have tools in social media that can be used to expand our business platform to reach customers directly. It is important to approach business on social media with an educated well-researched plan for growth. Facebook is the most popular and most used social media program that will accommodate a business platform using a page and a group. LinkedIn is set for business contacts. Individuals need to educate themselves to use technology hardware and software. Consumers that have grown to use social media are looking to be entertained and educated in a friendly, fun manner. Content must be delivered in an engaging, educating manner to expand group membership and entertain members. Seeking and courting influencers can help grow membership. All social media programs have their unique specialties and work best when their strengths are learned and utilized.

Key words: Digital Data and Technology, Facebook Pages and Groups, LinkedIn Platform, B2B commerce B2C commerce, Influential Group Growth, Marketing and Growing Your Group

JEL Classification: O33, M310, I12

Introduction

Technology had changed our world and to keep up we change our behavior and learn to use the technology. Digital Data allows independent business owners resources to get their message out to the world if they adapt their behavior to use the digital platform. There is the requirement that we study the digital environment and learn what we need to do to communicate effectively. Technology allows us to live in a new world of global communication. If we educate ourselves to using a digital platform, we can reach many customers and even once isolated corners of our world. Popular digital platforms include Linked-in and Facebook.

What is LinkedIn?

LinkedIn is a social networking designed for companies and individual professionals. "Its main objective is to put people in contact who are looking for work synergies and new professional or business opportunities." (E- commerce Nation. 2018) LinkedIn is considered the largest professional community worldwide and is designed to keep a network of professional or work contacts.

Why Facebook?

Facebook, as the largest social digital media platform designed to promote personal relationships, has over two billion monthly active users. When asked, "Why Facebook?" The answer becomes obvious. "Because hard working professionals are already there." Facebook offers formats that are user-friendly. Personal pages, business pages, groups, and messaging are all available at a touch. But it requires hardware to reach the program. Humans need to learn to use technological hardware. Then there is a learning curve to learn the program. Yet the reward is substantial. "There's a very good chance you'll be able to connect with your target audience through Facebook" (Lee 2018). "Never before have businesses been able to reach their customer base so easily and on so intimate a level." (Jenkins 2017).

How do Facebook and LinkedIn Compare?

Facebook is a social network, for sharing and engaging, like being with family and friends. LinkedIn was set up for recruiters and job searchers to have a forum for contact. LinkedIn has evolved but is mostly used by professionals. College graduates seeking white collar jobs use LinkedIn. Sales jobs are frequent. Blue collar jobs are not frequently seen.

Facebook is an example of B2C commerce selling products directly to the end-user targeting consumers by interest and demographic. Facebook business offers Business pages allowing active posting and engagement with customers. LinkedIn is an example of B2B commerce by selling to businesses, targeting Industry and job titles. Businesses use LinkedIn for company pages, job postings, entice talent, develop maintain conversations with customers, and lead to social media channels. Many more consumers visit Facebook and this increase advertising revenue for Facebook (Tech 2019).

Figure 1. *Facebook Versus LinkedIn*

	Facebook	LinkedIn
Members	Over 1.59 billion	Over 400 million
Monthly visitors	1 billion	100 million
Gender of visitors	43% male 57% female	50% male 50% female
Age of visitors	13-17 years: 7% 18-34 years: 26% 35+ years: 66%	13-17 years: 1% 18-34 years: 19% 35+ years: 80%

Source: Tech, 2019

Adapting Our Practices to Technology

Our elevator pitch which we are used to delivering in person, has transitioned to the "About" page in the digital media world of Facebook. This is a change in our behavior we have to learn to write our on -line profiles. Learn to offer your business using a pinned post to the top of your page that draws describes your business and group location. Make your page valuable for your visitor to "like" and follow your page (Jenkins 2017).

With technology and the internet we have search engines. We need to structure our wording to trigger the search engines. That way they will pull us up to be easier for our customers to find. Digital marketing guides us think of Facebook groups as communities This is a major change in our societies. We are used to going to group meetings in our communities. With technology we can attend groups and pod casts with anyone in the world.

Facebook groups are communities where one billion members share interests and goals using the Facebook's platform. "Think of groups run by other people as mini-communities. You can join up to 6,000 groups" (Cannon 2018). We extend our reach much broader than just our home community with Digital social media.

In groups set yourself as an expert and share your business with customers. This greatly extends your reach over just your local community. Share your expertise when you can. "If you can provide solutions, you and your business will become top-of-mind with members of the group. People start to look to you for answers by tagging you in comments" (Cannon 2018).

Technology is inexpensive compared to traditional methods of communication such as Mail, TV, or Billboards. Once the hardware is established social media software is inexpensive. "Imagine that you had a captive marketing audience. You could speak to them at any time, they would listen, and get excited when you told them about anything. They would stop whatever they were working on to listen to you and respond. And, this is the best part, when you asked them to buy your product or service, they would do so" (Patel 2010). When people come to your page or group if they are present and motivated, then you provide the trigger for the action you desire they take (Fogg 2007).

With technology you can build a community without borders. The digital world frees many limitations of the traditional world so you can reach further than ever before. "Build a community of people around you who believe in the same ideas and value what you do, you'll be able to foster new relationships with hundreds of new people who are open to learning from you" (Elkins 2017).

Still privacy and behavior must be protected. This requires a new skill set to protect ourselves and our customers. Digital media seems to bring out bullying as it feels anonymous, and individuals have committed suicide as a result of bullying. Consider a Facebook group as private where only members can view and discuss content. A Facebook page is public, anyone can view and comment.

Managing People Through Using Technology

Preparing and managing groups requires careful organized management. Folks are often separated when using technology. Techniques need to be learned to manage individuals you cannot see and known only as words and profiles. It is extremely important to be gracious and welcoming to those you meet on-line.

Teach your members what to do to participate and engage in your group. People are likely inexperienced in correct behaviors on-line and need to be taught how to behave for best results. Every user needs to feel important, and if you're able to do that, the group as a whole becomes a lot more valuable. "Above all, read and comment on member questions and interactions with other members" (Cannon 2018). "Demonstrate using Facebook notifications to keep up with activity in your group. Ask your group pointed questions and request members responses. Help your group members grow and teach them what you need from them in your group" (Patel 2016).

Even though we work to be proactive for problem solving, additional leaning skills are needed when used in technologies. "Be open, honest and helpful (especially if you encounter any problems that may occur with customers and users or if you receive any complaints)" (Veresearch 2020). Technology requires more transparency as all the customer has is what they see from technology. In 2018, Mark Zuckerberg, Facebook founder, expressed people want friendly messages from family and friends and warm interactions in groups. "Invite conversation whenever possible, with each post you do." (Marrs 2011). Communication is critical is when the person we are trying to reach is not present.

Figure 2. ***Use of Live Video***

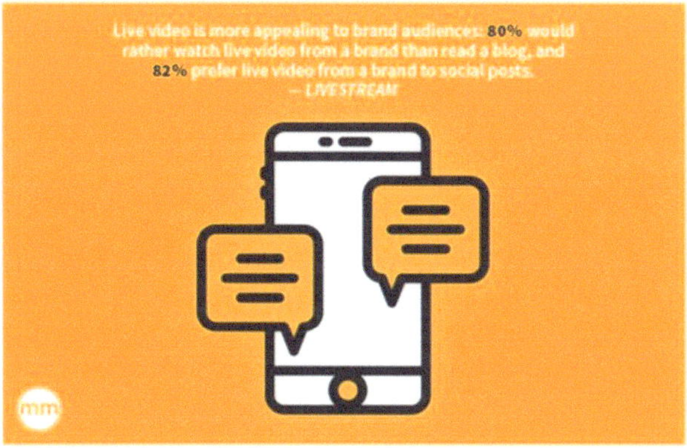

Source: Patel, 2016

A pure technological process, Facebook Video Marketing offers a personal feel and is "40 times more likely to get shared on social media than other types of content. People get excited and involved in videos. According to the social media channel's newsroom. People spend more than 3 times more time watching a Facebook Live video on average compared to a video that's no longer live" (Zantal-Weiner 2014).

Using Digital Communication

Send specific, customized messages to group members. "One successful way I discovered is sending personal messages to group members" (Patel 2016). This offers the illusion of value and privacy. The warm engaged feelings are important to foster in your group.

"One of the great things about groups is you can initiate a group chat/ message with either all members of a group or select members" (Ayers 2013). In past decades this level of contact required in person meetings. Encourage intense, passionate discussion.

"Inside the group you can create events that only members can see and RSVP" (Ayers 2013). Members attending events can share their impressions and network. "Be Interesting! Post fascinating stuff. Nobody, and I mean nobody, wants to look at a boring Facebook page" (Marrs 2011).

Managing Relationships When Using Technology

Even when using technology, the process is about building relationships. "Focus on using the real relationships you already have and deepen new ones before you start cold targeting people" (Elkins 2017). People like to feel wanted and helpful. Encourage the people you meet using technology to help you build your business platform.

A study conducted by The New York Time in 2016 found that people shared content on social media for 5 main reasons (Alton 2016):

1. To reveal valuable and entertaining content to others.
2. To define themselves to others.

3. To grow and nourish relationships.
4. For self-fulfillment.
5. To get the word out about brands and causes they like or support.

"Appeal to your group members' emotions by letting them know how much their sharing helps grow the group, and how much you appreciate it (Alton 2016). "The strong relationships you have with your advocates and brand ambassadors are invaluable." (Ayers 2013). By fostering relationships through technology, your platform and goodwill grows.
Another way to advance your technological projects is to get influencers in your niche to join your projects. As other people see that the influencer is a member, they may seek you out simply out of curiosity. Their thought process is that if the influencer is interested the project must be good! Influencer marketing can have a huge impact on your group's growth especially if you're just starting out. (Patel 2017).

We are used to having influencers in person. They come to meetings to help us influence others.
Now influencers can be utilized and contacted on-line by email and by video chat. They can help us in pod casts from their own homes by video to our customers.
Facebook is still high in social media use. "Facebook is still the king when it comes to user engagement. The average visit length is 20 minutes, with over half (55%) of all users logging in multiple times a day!" (Patel 2017). "One billion people visit Facebook Pages every month, four million 'likes' every minute, adding up to 250 million 'likes' every day" (Patel 2016). This can actively grow your Facebook presence successfully.
Technology goes where people live and can feel personal. Individuals can share expertise and teach others skills. Educate your people on how to behave for best results when using technology.
"Why not make it so that the reason these people check Facebook is to see what's going on in your group? Make sure posts that promote your group make it into your regular posting schedule on all your platforms. You can even tweet or mention other influencers to let them know you have a group that might be of interest to their followers. The content could be a free video training, a guide, a PDF checklist, you name it. When

you link over to special content that's found only in your group, you need to store it in your group" (Patel, 2017).

Conclusion

Technology had changed our world and to keep up we change our behavior and learn to use the technology. We live in a time when we can communicate directly with individual customers. We can reach parts of the world that were isolated during previous decades. We have tools in social media that can be used to expand our business platform to reach customers directly.

Digital Data allows independent business owners resources to get their message out to the world if they adapt their behavior to use the digital platform. There is the requirement that we study the digital environment and learn what we need to do to communicate effectively. Technology allows us to live in a new world of global communication. If we educate ourselves to using a digital platform, we can reach many customers and even once isolated corners of our world.

Bibliography

1. Anton, Larry. 2016. "Why-Do-People-Share-Content-a-Look-at-the-Psychology-of-Social-Sharing." Https://Socialnomics.Net. August 23, 2016.

2. Ayres, Scott. 2013. "How to Create a Facebook Group." Postplanner.Com. Post Planner. July 20, 2013. https://www.postplanner.com/how-to-create-a- facebook-group/.

3. "BJ Fogg, PhD Behavior Scientist at Stanford University." 2007. 2007. https://www.bjfogg.com.

4. Brent Barnhart. 2019a. "How the Facebook Algorithm Works and Ways to Outsmart It." Sprout Social. Brent Barnhart. May 31, 2019. https://sproutsocial.com/insights/facebook-algorithm/.

5. ———. 2019b. "Facebook Group Marketing: How to Build Your Community." Sprout Social. December 5, 2019. https://sproutsocial.com/insights/marketing-tips-facebook-groups/.

6. Cannon, Tammy. 2018. "How to Use Facebook Groups for Business: A Guide for Marketers." Social Media Marketing | Social Media Examiner. November 11, 2018.

https://www.socialmediaexaminer.com/facebook- groups-for-business-how-to-guide-for-marketers/.
7. Elkins, Lena. 2017. "The Truth About Facebook Group Marketing." Social

Media Today. March 31, 2017. https://www.socialmediatoday.com/social-networks/truth-about-facebook-group-marketing.

8. E-commerce Nation. 2018. "WHAT IS LINKEDIN, WHAT IS IT for and HOW DOES THIS PROFESSIONAL SOCIAL NETWORK WORK?" November 18, 2018. https://www.ecommerce-nation.com/what-is-linkedin-what-is-it-for-and-how- does-this-professional-social-network-work/.

9. Gotter, Ana. 2019. "Everything You Need to Know About Facebook Groups (2019 Update)." AdEspresso. September 12, 2019. https://adespresso.com/ blog/facebook-groups-everything-you-need-know/.

10. Jenkins, Lisa D. 2017. "Facebook Marketing: The Ultimate Guide to Facebook for Business." Social Media Marketing | Social Media Examiner. August 22, 2017. https://www.socialmediaexaminer.com/facebook- marketing-ultimate-guide-facebook-business/.

11. Lee, Kevan. 2018. "How to Create the Perfect Facebook Page for Your Business: The Complete A to Z Guide." Buffer Marketing Library. Buffer Social Blog. October 3, 2018. https://buffer.com/library/how-to-create-manage-facebook-business-page.

12. Main, Kelly. 2019. "How to Create a Facebook Business Page in 7 Steps." Fit Small Business. Fit Small Business. January 2, 2019. https:// fitsmallbusiness.com/how-to-create-a-facebook-business-page/.

13. Marrs, Megan. 2011. "10 Tips for Creating Content on Facebook That Gets the Thumbs Up." Wordstream.Com. 2011. https://www.wordstream.com/blog/ ws/2011/10/19/10-facebook-tips-for-content.

14. Odak, Petra. n.d. "7 Differences between B2B & B2C Ecommerce You Should Know." https://www.sendcloud.com/differences-b2b-b2c-ecommerce/.

15. Patel, Neil. 2010. "Facebook Marketing: A Comprehensive Guide for Beginners." Neil Patel. September 15, 2010. https://neilpatel.com/blog/ facebook-marketing/.

16. ———. 2016. "An Eye-Opening Guide on How to Grow a Facebook Group." Neil Patel. February 18, 2016. https://neilpatel.com/blog/an-eye-opening-guide-on-how-to-grow-a-facebook-group/.
17. ———. 2017. "How to Keep Your Facebook Group Active and Engaged." Neil Patel. March 12, 2017. https://neilpatel.com/blog/facebook-group- marketing/.

18. Sales & Marketing Technology (Tech). 2019. "The Differences between LinkedIn and Facebook for Business." March 12, 2019.
19. Zantal-Wiener, Amanda. 2014. "14 Essential Tips for an Engaging Facebook Business Page." Hubspot.Com. 2014. https://blog.hubspot.com/marketing/how-to-create-facebook-business-page-ht.

Contact information

Name of the author: Laura McCoy
Affiliation (University): LIGS University
Email: lmccy@wcc.net

Digital Data-ware House (ETL) Transformation and it's Cashless Economy

Aslam Mohamed Haneef

Abstract

Digital Data Transformation taking a turn into new era of technology toward digitalization and modernization. It represents state of the art for technology to be chosen for Banking operation and administration of data-driven business to be automated and well-organized in the digital formation. The key aspect of data-driven business for banks can be able to demonstrate physical and logical means of data to be distributed across all mediums in the banking media and marketing area of knowledge. The real question is about Digital Data-ware House Storage and Presentation application is able to manage such data in the current banking industry. Realistic Digital Data-ware House and its methodology is illustrated by taking creative surveys and their analytical for data transformation. It has simulated with typical example of Digital Data-ware House transformation case studies along with Bank's ETL process and automation of offline files to bank's various systems. Illustrated Scientific Study on the Future of Data-ware Housing and on clouds with the challenges of Legacy Data Warehousing, Data Warehouse Modernization and their goals, Data Warehousing and Hadoop.

Keywords: Corona Virus Disease 2019 (Covid-19), Credit Risk Rating (CRR), Enterprise Fraud Monitoring System (EFMS), Extract Transform and Load (ETL), Enterprise Service Bus (ESB), Financial Reporting and Analysis System (FRAS), Non Preforming Assets (NPA), Relationship Management System (RMS), Wealth Management System (WMS), T24 – Temenos Core Banking Product for Banking Solution (T24)

JEL Classification: C - C5 & C55, C - C8 & C81, F - F2 & F23, G - G15 & G21, N - N2 & N23 and Y - Y1 & Y10

Introduction

Digital Data transformation involves using digital technologies to remake a process to become more efficient or effective. The idea is to use technology not just to replicate an existing service in a digital form, but to use technology to transform that service into something significantly better.

Figure 1. ***Digital Dataware House Transformation Strategy***

Source: Zdnet - Mark Samuels, 2018

Digital data-ware house transformation and integration in banks will entail a variety of innovations, but the hottest topics right now in terms of current industry dynamics are Cloud computing, Internet of Things, Big data, and Artificial Intelligence (AI).

Figure 2. ***Technological Transformation for Business***

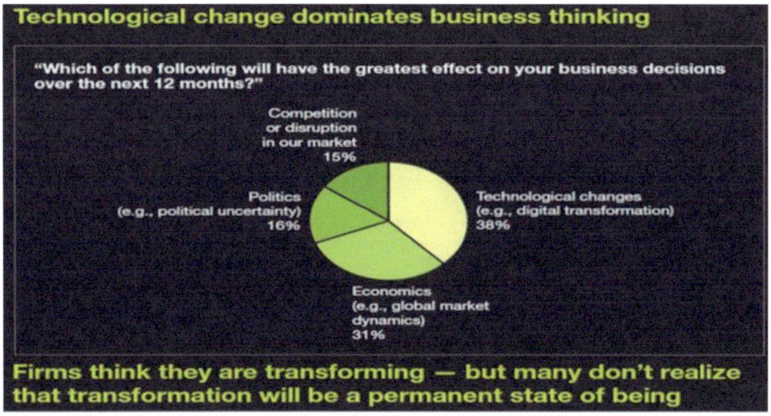

Source: Zdnet - Mark Samuels, 2018

However, changing market processes and organizational culture are equally important to the progress of these programs and subsequent processes. Digital development initiatives for banks are often used by big and existing banks to deal with quicker, digital-only competitors. These ventures are typically vast in scale and ambition, but they are not without risk. Although digital data transformation is one of the most often used and overused terms in the information technology industry, meanings vary. What everybody should agree on is that, under the hype, fluff, and misunderstanding, digital innovation entails some significant changes to the corporate ethos of today's technology (Zdnet, 2018)

Material – Data and Methodology

Worldwide spending on digital transformation technologies -- hardware, software, and services -- hit $1.3 trillion in 2017, according to IDC (MacTech.com, 2021). Between now and 2021, the overall amount invested on digitalization worldwide is expected to almost double, surpassing the fund of $2.1 trillion, according to a tech consulting firm (ZDNet, 2021). In a survey of 460 executives conducted by IT analyst Gartner, 62% have a management plan or transition program in place to make banks more digitalize (Solvera, 2021). Just over half (54%) stated that their digital business goal is transformational, while 46% stated that the initiative's goal is optimization for those banks (Solvera, 2021).

Figure 3. ***Executive Attitudes to Business Transformation***

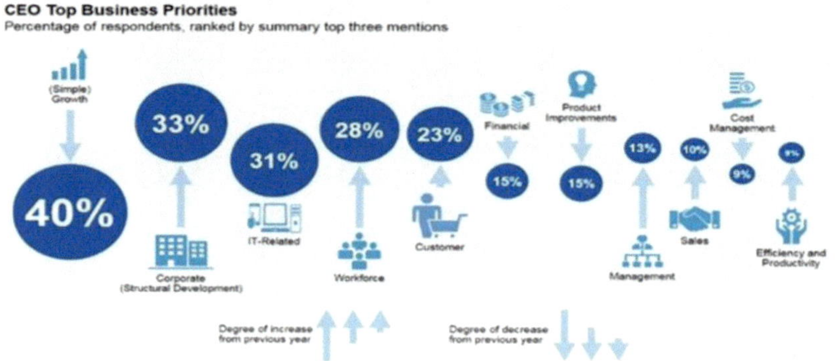

Source: Zdnet - Mark Samuels, 2018

According to a new Grant Thornton poll, more than two-thirds (69%) of CFOs and senior financial executives expect to increase their spending in developments that accelerate market improvements in the next 12 months, with four in ten expecting an increase of more than 10%. Just under half of respondents said their businesses' investments in digital transformation are intended to help them outperform their competitors by differentiation (CFO South Africa, 2020). The World Economic Forum estimates that the potential of digital change for society and business will surpass $100 trillion by 2025, but it is not just positive news (Linked.in, 2021). According to Forrester, digital transformation attempts are obstructed by misunderstanding, misinformation, and resistance to transition (Zdnet, 2018).

Digital Data transformation examples – Case Studies

McDermott International is creating a digital twin, which is a computer model of the oil and gas platform facilities which provides to clients. The firm foresees 15 percent boost to operational margins by using the design- twin approach in key areas like predictive maintenance and Gartner believes half of industrial firms will use digital twins by coming years (ITPFED, 2020).

Rolls Royce's R² Data Labs initiative uses machine learning (ML), AI and data analytics to create new services. The R² Data Labs team, which includes 200 data architects, engineers, scientists and specialist mangers have helped Rolls-Royce deliver more than £250m in value through engine-health monitoring activities in the past 12 months and so (Autactics, 2019).

Logistics firm UPS is placing analytics and insight at the heart of business operations. The firm is using real-time data, advanced analytics and AI to help employees make better decisions and firm recently launched third iteration of its chatbot that uses AI to help customers find rates and tracking information subsequently (ITPFED, 2020).

When does digital data transformation stop?

It does not, and many people make the mistake of seeing digital data transformation as a standalone endeavor. True transition, as Forrester says, is a journey rather than a destination (Celagenix, 2021). Digital transformation is still a hazy phenomenon that entails providing value to businesses and their customers in novel and perhaps unconventional ways (Celagenix, 2021). Despite the fact that appetite for change will continue to change or emerge as fresh, 21% of market and technology decision makers think their digital transformation strategies are already complete (Zdnet, 2018).

Scientific Research and Simulation of Data-ware House (ETL) into various Bank's Application Systems

Banks are implementing and transforming the place of replacing its Legacy application with T24 systems for its Digital Core Banking Solution. As part of the expansion of the Bank's Technical Architecture landscape and the transformation digital data-ware house initiative, the banks chosen for ETL (Extract, Transform and Load) method extracts for majority of the bank's current extracting requirements and their storage. This effectively means that T24 system will be providing consolidated ETL Extracts for the extracting requirements identified through various interface elements such as and not limited to as follows.

- BASEL2 Extracts
- CRR Extracts
- RMS and WMS Batch Interface
- FRAS Extracts
- EFMS and Sanctions Extracts
- Kondor System Extracts

ETL extract is a build-up approach, means in this approach of T24 ETL extraction of consolidated extracts on business work-stream applications from various tables of T24 System, as stated below.

- Basel2 Deposits Extract – Monthly Consolidated Extract
- Basel2 Loans – Monthly Consolidated Extract
- Basel2 Islamic Loans – Monthly Consolidated Extract

- Basel2 Mortgage (MTG) – Monthly Consolidated Extract
- Basel2 NPA – Monthly Consolidated Extract
- Basel2 PF – Monthly Consolidated Extract
- Basel2 SG – Monthly Consolidated Extract
- Money Market – Daily Extract – Conventional Deposits
- Loans and Deposit – Daily Extract – Islamic Deposits
- Loans and Deposit – Daily Extract – Islamic Murabaha Deposits

The Current new process of T24 System is to take care of ETL Consolidated Extracts from T24 through delimited file for both cycles as stated below.

- Incremental Daily Extract – Daily Incremental Updates as applicable
- Monthly Extract – Full Dump data extracts as applicable

File Transportation Mode of Integration is Offline i.e., by batch mode Integration of file.

File Format is Delimited Text File i.e., by file format is delimited by special character by fields

Figure 4. ***Architecture Overview of T24 ETL***

Source: Temenos Internals - Aslam Mohamed, 2014

Overview of FRAS Interface from T24 to ETL

Financial Reporting Analysis System (FRAS) requires data that resides in the core banking system in order to generate financial reports for analysis and regulatory. FRAS will need data-ware house to be provided on daily and monthly basis (Batches). As T24 will replace Bank's legacy core banking system, information that the FRAS used to get from legacy will now be generated from T24. FRAS can get the needed data through processing T24 generated batch files. Batch files are generated by T24 and moved to Bank's ETL which would provide the same files to FRAS. ETL will be transforming the files to the FRAS format. T24 will be generating batch files for the required extract.

Figure 5. ***T24 System Interface Extraction for FRAS System***

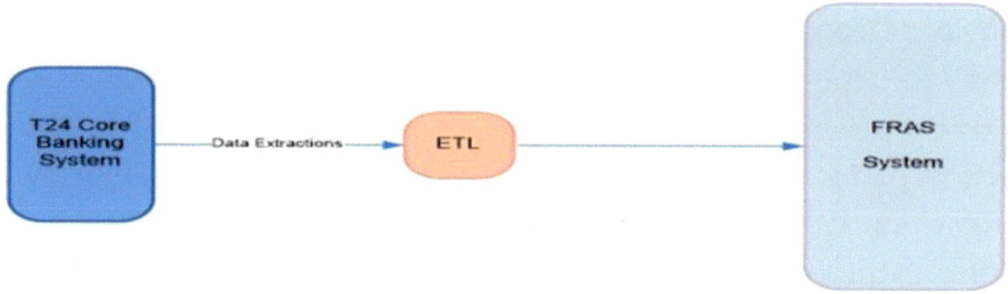

Source: SNB Bank Internals - Aslam Mohamed, 2017

The consolidated files will be provided to ETL which would provide the required target files in the needed format to FRAS. In case a non ETL approach is selected, the below file details will be applied while generating the file. The batch files needed for the FRAS and the content are listed below.

- Customer
- Account
- EOD Balances
- Daily Transactions
- Deposits
- Loans
- Trade Products
- Loan Repayment
- Central Liability

The below table contains the list of batch services:

Table 1.

S.N	Stage of Data Extracted	Source	Operation Performs	Mode of Operation	Frequency	Message Type
1	Customer	T24	ETL Extract	Offline	Incremental Daily	CSV File.
2	Account	T24	ETL Extract	Offline	Incremental Daily	CSV File.
3	EOD Balances	T24	ETL Extract	Offline	Daily & On Demand	CSV File.
4	Daily Transactions	T24	ETL Extract	Offline	Daily	CSV File.
5	Deposits	T24	ETL Extract	Offline	Daily	CSV File.
6	Loans	T24	ETL Extract	Offline	Daily	CSV File.
7	Loan Repayment	T24	ETL Extract	Offline	Daily	CSV File.
8	Trade Products	T24	ETL Extract	Offline	Daily	CSV File.

Source: SNB Bank Internals - Aslam Mohamed, 2017

Loans Details Extracts – Sample Example

The purpose of this service is to perform operation of extracting files from the T24 to specific folder with specific file name. This extraction will contain all Loans (Corporate, Retail & Islamic) records from LD.LOANS.AND.DEPOSITS table. The field extraction will be as per the requirement given in the attached shown below. The mapping details are available under the attached below under Daily Loan Details Extract heading.

Table 2.

Type of Operation	Description
Service Type	This is a batch/online service (Batch ETL Extraction)
Direction	Daily Extraction from T24 to FRAS
Frequency	Full Extract Daily basis.
File Characteristics	Comma "," delimited CSV file.
File Naming Convention.	FRAS_<COMP>_DLYLOAN_T24_YYYYMMDD.csv
Multi Company Processing	Individual files should be provided for each LEAD Company.
Selection Criteria	Select all the records which are LIVE and all the records which are MATURING during the month from the LD.LOANS.AND.DEPOSITS table with CATEGORY ranging from 21050 to 21074.

Source: SNB Bank Internals - Aslam Mohamed, 2017

Scientific Study on the Future of Data-ware Housing and Data-ware House on clouds

Data Management - Self-service, Big data, Data lakes, NoSQL, Hadoop, and the cloud raise questions about the role of the data warehouse in modern analytic ecosystems. Though experts have declared that the data warehouse dead, most organizations continue to operate at least one data warehouse, with the majority operating two to five, and expect to do so for the foreseeable future. Data warehousing is alive, but perhaps not alive and well (Cloudera - The Future of Data Warehousing, 2018).

Data Warehousing is Not Dead

Despite expert assertions, data warehousing is not dead. According to recent research, more than 60% of businesses nowadays operate between two and five data warehouses. Fewer than 10% have a single data warehouse or none at all. Almost one-third of those polled work in a company that has six or more data warehouses. Although the previous generation's ideal of BI and data warehousing, of a single data warehouse serving as a single version of the truth, has not been achieved, it is apparent that data warehousing continues to give value to these businesses. Data warehouses suit people's information demands and continue to give value, and many people rely on them and do not want them to be replaced by a data lake. Data lakes meet the demands of analytics and big data, and they provide a rich source of data for data scientists and self-service data consumers (Cloudera - The Future of Data Warehousing, 2018).

The Challenges of Legacy Data Warehousing

Data warehousing is not dead, but it is struggling, and it is alive but perhaps not entirely well. Legacy data warehousing is being challenged by big data, NoSQL, data science, self-service analytics, and the requirement for speed and agility. Traditional data warehousing, which is based on data management approaches from the 1990s, simply cannot keep up with the demands of ever increasing data quantities, processing workloads, and data analysis use cases. To meet the reality of modern data management and address the issues of scalability and elasticity, data diversity, data latency, adaptability, data silos, and data science compatibility, data warehousing must change and adapt (Cloudera - The Future of Data Warehousing, 2018).

Data Warehouse Modernization

Data warehousing badly need modernization and overcoming the challenges described here can only be achieved by rethinking the architecture, design, and implementation of data warehouses. Modernization is required if data warehousing is to stay up with business changes, shorten data-to-insight times, and adapt to other regulatory requirements. With the numerous issues of historical data warehousing, it is tempting to pronounce the data warehouse dead and migrate to a data lake. Avoid the temptation since it isn't a genuine or practical answer. The data lake is not a panacea; it is an important source of data for many analytics use cases; nevertheless, it is not meant to be subject-oriented, integrated, non-volatile, and time-variant, and hence is not well positioned to offer the benefits of data warehousing. A data lake and data warehousing working together in a data management ecosystem that offers the proper data for the complete spectrum of use cases, from simple reporting to advanced analytics and data science, is the optimal answer. To get that ideal solution, historical data warehouses must be architecturally, operationally, and technologically modernized. Modernization of data warehouses is required, but it can be difficult. Knowledge and comprehension, uninterrupted operations, and architectural inadequacies are all major challenges (Cloudera - The Future of Data Warehousing, 2018).

The Goals of Modernization

Data warehouse modernization is a purposeful undertaking to achieve specific and tangible benefits that improve data management, enhance data value, and drive positive business impact. Those benefits include:

- A complete and cohesive analytics ecosystem
- Complete and cohesive data management architecture
- Maximum reusability and reuse
- Data for all
- Technological updates
- Architectural updates
- Automation opportunities

Top Data Warehouse Software's

- Snowflake
- BigQuery
- Vertica
- Microsoft
- Teradata Vantage
- IBM Netezza
- Rubrik

Figure 6. ***Architectural Framework for Modern Data Management***

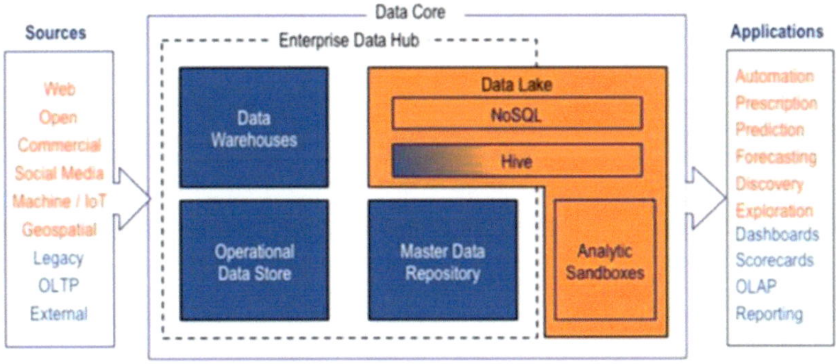

Source: Cloudera - Corinium, 2018

There is no one-size-fits-all approach for data warehouse modernization, and because each historical data warehouse is unique, each modernization strategy is also unique. However, there are various design patterns for contemporary data warehousing that might help to bridge the gap between present and future-state data warehouse goals. Architectural frameworks, cloud data warehousing, automation and virtualization, Hadoop data warehousing, and adoption of newly emerging technologies are all common trends. Follow these principles singly or in combination to create a modernization strategy and a framework for your contemporary data warehouse architecture (Cloudera - The Future of Data Warehousing, 2018).

Data Warehousing in the Cloud

Cloud data warehousing has grown in popularity as businesses face increasing data quantities, rising service level requirements, and the need to connect structured warehouse data with unstructured data in a data lake. The shift to SaaS for corporate applications makes cloud data warehousing a more appealing choice. Many of the historical data warehouse difficulties are addressed by cloud data warehousing, which provides a specific and direct answer to the difficulties of scalability, flexibility, performance, and workload control. Less obvious but no less essential advantages include easy access to technologies optimized for non-relational and unstructured data, increased flexibility and agility through immediate infrastructure, and less reliance on on-premises data centers for cost efficient management (Cloudera - The Future of Data Warehousing, 2018).

Migrating Legacy Data Warehouses to the Cloud - Migrating an existing data warehouse to the cloud has substantial benefits and is a practical step to modernization, but it is not quick or easy. Tactically and technically, data warehouse migration is a challenging multi-step process to move many different warehousing components.

Figure 7. *Migrating a Data Warehouse to the Cloud*

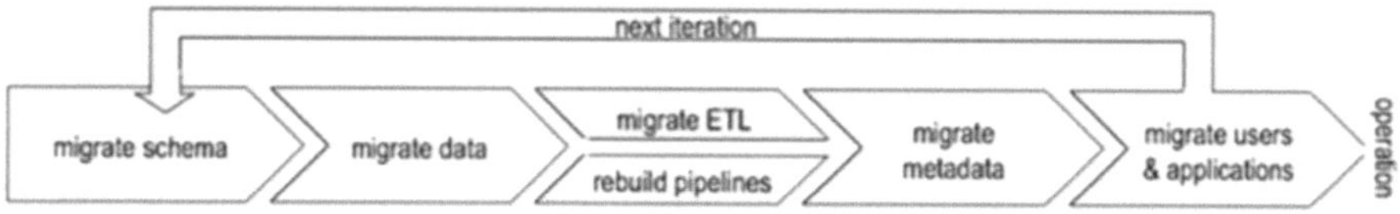

Source: Cloudera - Corinium, 2018

Data Warehousing and Hadoop

Hadoop is frequently used as a big data and data lake solution. It is reasonable for enterprises that have invested in Hadoop deployment and skill development to wonder how Hadoop might help with data warehouse transformation. When scalability, flexibility, and database capacity are among the legacy data warehousing concerns, Hadoop is a feasible option (Cloudera - The Future of Data Warehousing, 2018).

Results / Discussion

The COVID-19 pandemic crisis has acted as a force for transition, with what we once thought "natural" in the workplace and culture at large perhaps never returning. From handshakes to head nods, open office to working from home, face-to-face meetings to Zoom, and physical cash payment to digital payment solutions, eliminating contact from our communications and purchases has become a required precaution in order to try and control the spread of the novel coronavirus (Emerging Payments UK, 2020).

When COVID-19 infections increased and cases spread from country to country, the World Health Organization (WHO) recommended that you wash your hands after handling currency. While no formal ties have been established between cash handling and potential COVID-19 transmission, we were advised to improve our personal hygiene practices. Many companies now choose to request contactless payments from consumers, whether via payment card or mobile services. To name a handful, supermarkets, courier services, and taxis which is within weeks, the trend had shifted to card and smartphone payments, and financial institutions replied by lifting limits on contactless purchases, such as the contactless payment cap in the United Kingdom from £30 to £45 (Emerging Payments UK, 2020).

According to research undertaken by the data firm Dynata, United Kingdom is heading the drive to go cashless. According to a new poll, while 12 percent of UK people still favor cash payments, 50 percent of residents said they favored cashless payments prior to COVID-19, this has now risen to 59 percent. The preference for contactless and cashless payments continues to be on the rise in Europe (Emerging Payments UK, 2020).

Figure 8. ***Cashless Payment across Europe***

Payment by Contactless Debit or Credit Card	UK	59%	Contactless Payment App on a phone	UK	9%
	Netherlands	57%		Germany	8%
	France	52%		Netherlands	8%
	Italy	41%		Spain	7%
	Spain	39%		Italy	5%
	Germany	35%		France	5%

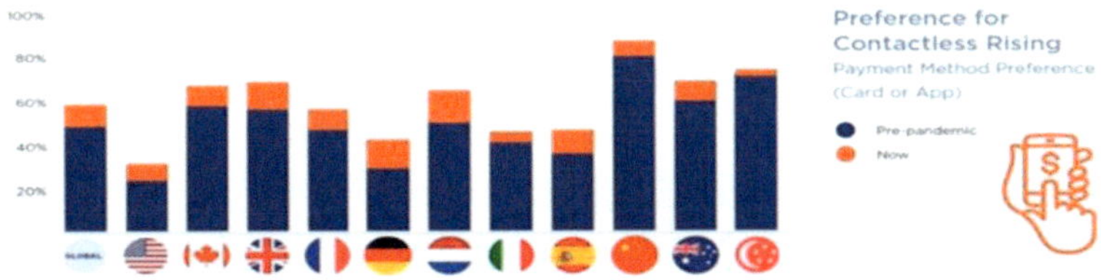

Source: Emerging Payments UK - Charlie Osborne, 2020

"Across all the markets, highest level of contactless payment ownership pre-pandemic was seen in China at 90%, followed by Singapore with 85% owning some form of contactless card or phone app, UK (81%) and Australia (78%)," the report notes. "In USA, by contrast, less than four in ten [38%] had contactless methods of payment before the pandemic, much lower than the global average of 68%." The report says that now, in the United States, there has been a 19% increase in consumers' ability to access a form of contactless payment method, joining traditional options such as cash, signatures and stripes, and chip-and-pin (Emerging Payments UK, 2020).

Conclusion Summary

The real question is about Digital Data-ware House Storage and Presentation application is able to manage such data in the current banking industry.

Digital Data-ware House Storage and Presentation Layers of Business Objects will be facing significant problem with the performance of the Digital data which is storage (5TB in Size) in the central server of the bank which have to be fine-tuned as well as stability for future purpose. The Database like Oracle, My-SQL, MS-SQL etc., which acts has data-ware house products will be playing a real role of digital data for easy accessibility of information so that it can enable and support Business Intelligence(BI) Products especially analytics area of scope. Digital Data-ware houses to perform queries and analysis which often contain large amount of historical or archival data from the databases. It has capability to centralizes and consolidate large amounts of data from multiple databases and analytical capabilities allow organizations to deliver valuable insights from their databases to improve decision making by the management. The evolution of Data-ware house from analytics to Artificial Intelligence (AI) and Machine Learning (ML) is the wide aspect and scope of Digital Data-ware house transformation and its strategy to take place in the nearby future.

Cashless or Contactless

Consumers were forced to change their buying patterns as a result of the accelerated spread of COVID-19, and financial institutions and brokers were forced to reconsider how they welcome payment. It is not the time to withdraw banknotes and coins from our pockets, but it seems that they

will disappear at some stage in the future as people get more used to and familiar with digital services, virtual wallets, and online banking. It is not just the generation who has grown up with broadband and mobile technologies that must be considered, and if cash is not secured, we risk isolating and hurting those who, for whatever cause, need physical money in their daily lives.
Coronavirus Impact Survey from The Employer Association – Interesting to read on to the current situation of COVID-19 crisis (Emerging Payments UK, 2020).

"Any device that gives you back your precious time is always going to be a hit, which is why we see more people making contactless payments and it's simply easier than cash," says Sukhi Jutla, co-founder of Market Orders. "With cash, you have to visit bank or an ATM to take cash out, and when you spend it you have to wait to get your change back and then carry those coins in your pockets. Without a doubt, we are moving towards a cashless society with millions of us using contactless cards or our smartphones and watches to simply tap and go."

Final words on Data ware Modernization

Data warehouse modernization is a journey, not an event. Done well it is a planned and incremental step-by-step process of moving from warehousing of the past to the future of data warehousing. Assess your current state of data warehousing and define your needs, challenges and prioritize them to know which are most pressing and need earliest attention. Define your future state of data warehousing as well as define then describe your goals for modernization with enough clarity to know when the goals have been achieved. Choose the modernization patterns that are best suited to your goals. Do not hesitate to mix and match patterns and might, for example, want to use data warehouse automation to reverse engineer a legacy data warehouse and then migrate that warehouse to the cloud or you might migrate a high use data warehouse to the cloud and federate other warehouses to break down the silos.

References/Bibliography

1. Mr. Mark Samuels, "What is digital transformation? Everything you need to know about how technology is reshaping business", Zdnet Article, May 2018, <https://www.zdnet.com/article/what-is-digital-transformation- everything-you-need-to-know-about-how-technology-is-reshaping/>
2. "IDC: digital transformation tech spending to hit $1.3 trillion in 2018", MacTech.com, May 2021, December 27, 2017, <https:// www.mactech.com/2017/12/27/idc-digital-transformation-tech-spending-to-hit-1-3-trillion-in-2018/>
3. "Using the cloud as a platform for digital transformation", ZDNet, May 2021, October 26, 2018, < https://www.zdnet.com/article/using-the- cloud-as-a-platform-for-digital-transformation/>
4. "What is digital transformation? Everything you need to know about how technology is reshaping business", Solvera, May 2021, <https:// solvera.id/2019/05/what-is-digital-transformation/>
5. "CFOs increase spending on digital transformation, seek competitive edge – survey", CFO South Africa, September 2020, <https://cfo.co.za/ articles/cfos-increase-spending-on-digital-transformation-seek- competitive-edge-survey/>
6. "What is Digital Transformation & Why It's Important ...", Linked.in, 2021, < https://www.linkedin.com/pulse/what-digital- transformation-why-its-important-pete-peranzo>
7. "Are You Ready For Hyperautomation?", ITPFED, January 2020, <https://itpfed.com/are-you-ready-for-hyperautomation/>
8. "Everything you need to know about how technology is reshaping business - MUST READ Autactics - Course Hero", Autactics, August 2019, < https://www.coursehero.com/file/44703314/Everything-you-need-to- know-about-how-technology-is-reshaping-businesspdf/>
9. "Digital Transformation – Rewriting The Rules Of Business", ITPFED, May 15, 2020, < https://itpfed.com/digital-transformation-rewriting-the-rules-of-business/>

10. "Five winning plays for digital transformation", Celagenix, January 2021, <https://celagenix.com/five-winning-plays-for-digital-transformation/>

11. "Cloudera - The Future of Data Warehousing", Cloudera - The Future of Data Warehousing, November 2018, https://www.coriniumintelligence.com/ insights/cloudera-the-future-of-data-warehousing>
12. "Coronavirus and a cashless society: We can't leave the most vulnerable behind", Emerging Payments UK, July 2020, <https:// www.emergingpayments.org/article/coronavirus-and-a-cashless-society-we-cant-leave-the-most-vulnerable-behind/> >
13. Mr. Aslam Mohamed, "Bank Integration Document", Temenos Internals, January 15-2014. January 2014, Temenos Internal Corporate Document, <https://www.temenos.com/>
14. Mr. Aslam Mohamed, "T24 System Interface Extraction of FRAS System", SNB Bank Internals, March 2017, Bank and Temenos Internal Document, <https://www.samba.com/en/personal-banking/ index.aspx> <https://www.ncbsambastronger.com/english>
15. Mr. Dave Wells, "The Future of Data Warehousing - Integrating with Data Lakes, Cloud, and Self-Service", DBTA Article, August 25 - 2018. September 2018, <https://www.dbta.com/DBTA-Downloads/WhitePapers/ The-Future-of-Data-Warehousing-8457.aspx>
16. The Employers Association, "Coronavirus Impact Survey", 3020 W. Arrowood Road – Charlotte - NC 28272, April 6 – 2020, <https:// www.employersassoc.com>

Contact information
Name of the author: Aslam Mohamed Haneef, Ph.D.
Affiliation (University): LIGS University
Email: aslam_1976@hotmail.com

Implications of Digital Technologies for Healthcare and Human Behavior

Adinet Lock

Abstract

The objective of this paper is to explore the use of digital technologies in healthcare, and provide a narrative review of the implications of these technologies for human behavior and health technology reimbursement. Digital technology, economy, and health specific sources were searched for this narrative review. Artificial Intelligence (AI) has been used to read and assess financial documents and reports, and extract data. As a result, some organizations have started to tailor their reports based on machine readability to generate a favorable outcome. In healthcare, lengthy dossiers are often developed to support decision-making about reimbursement during health technology assessments (HTAs). Similar to the financial sector, AI may play a role in future in how dossiers are written and assessed, and humans may be changing their behavior and writing style to achieve a desired outcome,

i.e. a positive reimbursement decision. This could have implications for stakeholders, and the quality of the algorithms used could either enhance the HTA process or result in large errors and costs to various stakeholders. Using AI for HTAs can save time and allow for the efficient evaluation of large amounts of data. However, high quality data and adequate evaluation of algorithms are needed to minimize bias and manipulation.

Keywords: digital technologies, health technology assessments, reimbursement

JEL Classification: I130, I180, H51

Introduction

There are a wide variety of definitions for the digital economy (Bukht & Heeks, 2017), but broadly it can be seen as a combination of digital equipment, technologies and skills as inputs that result in outputs such as "digital goods or services" (p. 5) (UNCTAD, 2019). Digital technologies and the digital economy are constantly evolving and expanding, and this is part of the reason why it is so hard to define (UNCTAD, 2019). The financial sector and economy is highly dependent on data, and has been impacted and changed as a result of data digitalisation (Johnstone et al., 2019). The digitalisation of data, big data and artificial intelligence (AI) enabled e-commerce, FinTech, and monitoring of financial flows at a high level, scale, speed and frequency (Johnstone et al., 2019). It has also resulted in increased complexity and created problems with regulation that requires advanced analytics (Johnstone et al., 2019). The financial sector consists of certain activities and services such as communications, funding, insurance, payment, planning, and security, and it uses digital technologies to perform these activities and provide these services (Johnstone et al., 2019). Technologies include AI, augmented reality (AR), virtual reality (VR), big data, biometric technology, 5G broadband, distributed ledger technology (blockchain), cloud computing (for example RegTech), robotics, and the Internet of Things (IoT) (Johnstone et al., 2019; UNCTAD, 2019). Apart from the financial sector, several other sectors make use of digital technologies and contribute to the digital economy, including technology services, consumer goods and services, and healthcare (UNCTAD, 2019). Many digital technologies are currently in use in healthcare. Although much has been written about the clinical applications of digital technologies in healthcare, there are also some economic applications that are connected to clinical, professional, and human issues (Alami et al., 2020). The objective of this paper is to explore the use of digital technologies in healthcare, and provide a narrative review of the implications of these technologies for human behavior and the digital economy in terms of health technology reimbursement.

Material and Methods

Digital technology, economy, and health specific sources were searched for relevant publications for this narrative review. Sources include the OECD library, the International Journal of Digital Technology & Economy, the Journal of Economic Literature, Technology and Society, The Journal of Medical Internet Research, United Nations reports, the Economic & Social

Research Council, and a few economic consulting firm websites. First, broad search terms such as "digital economy" were used to identify studies for background information (Appendix I). Second, more specific terms and combinations were used and hand searches were conducted to indentify sources which specifically address digital technologies and their application in health care and for the reimbursement of health interventions.

Results and Discussion

Technologies already in use in healthcare

In healthcare, technologies such as advanced computational approaches, blockchain, online verification, mobile and radio frequency are used (Johnstone et al., 2019). For example, AR and VR can improve the capability to communicate, learn, interact and visualize information in 3D (Mustonen, 2020; TECHNOSTACKS, 2021). E-healthcare, includes electronic prescriptions and records, telemedicine, and exchange of medical data online (European Commission, 2020b). Data sources that play a role in increasing efficiency includes AI and big data (European Commission, 2020b). AI has the potential to improve the accuracy of diagnosis, improve disease prevention, and improve healthcare delivery (European Commission, 2020c). However, one study found that there was substantial variation in diagnostic accuracy between AI platforms (Aboueid et al., 2019). Large amounts of data can be rapidly processed and analyzed with big data to produce results in different formats in real-time (European Commission, 2020b). IBM's Watson uses AI, blockchain, and cloud for various applications in health including clinical decision-making (via electronic health records, diagnostics, medication and disease information), and exchanging data with payers (IBM, 2021; UNCTAD, 2019). There are also a few newer technologies including "high performance computing (HPC)" (p. 83) that have implications for the economy and healthcare (European Commission, 2020b). HPC can be used to overcome and respond to many challenges because it consists of supercomputers that can address very complex problems involving large data sets and a high level of computational ability (European Commission, 2020b). HPC can also be combined with AI, big data and cloud computing (European Commission,

2020b). Health technology manufacturers can use data to develop, improve and sell their products, and to improve the efficiency of their processes (Nguyen & Paczos, 2020). Examples of how data and digital technologies have improved processes include combating counterfeit medications by using bar codes to confirm authentication; using big data and medical health records to reduce the time and cost of randomized controlled trials (RCTs); online tools such as Predictiv makes RCT pilot testing easy; and big data can provide access to a much larger data set and can improve health surveillance (Johnstone et al., 2019). However, it has also failed in predicting things like a flu-season or trend which shows its limitations and that big data can be plagued by "big error" (p. 22) (Johnstone et al., 2019). Table 1 lists digital technologies, their uses in healthcare, and how it can potentially affect behavior.

Table 1. ***Digital technologies and Their Application and Impact in Health Systems***

Digital technologies	Healthcare use	Potential behavior change
Artificial Intelligence	Improve accuracy of diagnosis, disease prevention and health care delivery, and evidence assessment	Reliance on technology rather than skills and experience, possible uncertainty if conflict
Augmented & Virtual Reality	Communicate, learn, interact, visualise in 3D, medical training	Depersonalization, impaired perception, cyber sickness
Big data	Rapid analysis and processing of large data sets, real-time results, evidence assessment	Change the way we work and how decisions are made
Biometric technology	Identifying patients and securely sharing their data, telemedicine and mobile medication dispensing	Personalized but not personal, self-monitoring, fear of profiling
5G broadband	Telemedicine, e-health platforms	Virtual rather than in-person; connected but disengaged
Distributed ledger technology (bitcoin, blockchain)	Exchanging data with payers; authentication of medications and fraud detection of counterfeit medications; medication reimbursement	Improve efficiency, self-authentication, increase transparency and trust
Cloud computing	Electronic health records, prescriptions, exchanging medical data online, systematic literature reviews	Improve collaboration, flexibility and data sharing
Robotics	Surgeries	Reduce errors and increase confidence & conditioning
Internet of Things	Remote patient monitoring through connected devices in real-time, smart sensors, wearables, randomized controlled trials, evidence assessment	Motivation to change and act, conditioning and increase willingness to share personal data
High performance computing	Solve very complex problems, genomic sequencing, clinical trials, health technology assessments	Increased accuracy and trust, black box, reduced understanding

Sources: Adapted from AWARE 2021 (AWARE, 2021); TheHealthcareInsights n.d.(Applications of Internet of Things in Healthcare); Mustonen 2020 (Mustonen, 2020); TECHNOSTACKS 2021 (TECHNOSTACKS, 2021); European Commission 2020 (European Commission, 2020b); European Commission 2020 (European Commission, 2020c); UNCTAD 2019 (UNCTAD, 2019); IBM 2021 (IBM, 2021); Bukht & Heeks 2017 (Bukht & Heeks, 2017); Hilty et al. 2020 (HIlty et al., 2020)

Communications, funding, payment and insurance are some financial activities and services that are applicable to healthcare. The European Open Science Cloud is involved in creating a health data space with the goal of improving the healthcare system in terms of access, efficacy, evidence-based decision-making and sustainability (European Commission, 2020a). In order for health systems to be sustainable, resources must be used optimally. Improved data and access to data can help regulatory bodies to better assess the efficacy and safety of health technologies such as medications and medical devices (European Commission, 2020a).

Health technology assessment and reimbursement process

Bringing health technologies to market and making them accessible to patients involve a life cycle consisting of several phases, processes and stakeholders. The processes are similar to that found in project management and includes initiation, planning, execution, monitoring, controlling and closing (Project Management Institute, 2017). Stakeholders include product developers (manufacturers/pharmaceutical companies), regulatory authorities, and Health Technology Assessment (HTA) agencies (Bujar, 2018). A health technology move through several stages where key decisions need to be made about whether to continue or stop – also referred to as a stage- gate approach (Ajam & bookboon.com, 2019; Bujar, 2018). At each milestone or gate, quality is assessed and next steps are determined (Van Der Schouw, 2015). Health technologies are subject to regulatory approval by regulatory agencies such as the European Medicines Agency (EMA). Once a medication or medical device is approved, it undergoes a formal Health Technology Assessment (HTA) to take its efficacy and cost (amongst other factors) into consideration and advise decision-makers on how to best prioritize and efficiently allocate limited resources (Bujar, 2018; ICER, 2018). Although not required in all countries, many countries use HTAs to decide whether to use public funds to pay for expensive new health technologies (ICER, 2018). HTAs are also used by doctors and patients to make decisions about treatments, and by researchers to identify lack of knowledge or gaps in evidence (ICER, 2018). HTA agencies assess medications from an economic, ethical and social perspective and take budget impact, comparative-effectiveness, and cost-effectiveness into consideration in order to make a decision about reimbursement (Bujar, 2018). HTA agencies and manufacturers, with the help of health economic and outcomes research (HEOR) companies, often develop dossiers to support decision-making and improve market access (Bujar, 2018; Khan et al., 2019). These dossiers can be hundreds of pages in length, and writing and reviewing them is very labour intensive. Dossier development and HTAs rely on systematic literature reviews (SLR) to find the most relevant and best available evidence to answer certain questions and make the best decisions (Adeva et al., 2014; Bujar, 2018). SLRs can sometimes produce thousands of articles that need to be screened and reviewed for relevancy and quality. There is an opportunity for AI and machine learning algorithms to play a role in the development and assessment of these dossiers. For example, machine learning algorithms (which is part of AI) have been used to screen titles and abstracts, and performed relatively well in terms of precision, sensitivity and specificity (Adeva et al., 2014; Popoff et al., 2020). Well-performing algorithms can cut down substantially on the time and people needed to perform SLRs. Additionally, AI may have implications for those who develop and assess health technology dossiers. AI has been used to read and assess financial documents and reports, and extract data from them (Naughton, 2020). It can also learn rules, perform auditing, pick up on non-compliant content to reduce reimbursement errors and waste (Shan, 2020). Algorithms are often making recommendations for what shares to buy or sell based on large-scale automated machine-learning computational processes "that identify positive, negative, and neutral opinions" (p. 2) from news and public reports and disclosures (Cao et al., 2020). In the financial sector, some organizations have started to tailor their reports based on "machine readability" (webpage) by using or not using words that would be interpreted as positive or negative, respectively, by an algorithm in order to generate a favourable outcome and conclusion about the content (Naughton, 2020). In other words, humans are changing their behavior, writing style, and content used in order for their work to be perceived positively by AI. Should this approach be applied to assess health technology dossiers, it could have implications for the people involved in developing these dossiers. Dossier developers may look at the dossiers of similar health technologies which have received a positive reimbursement decision and extract "positive words" to include in their own dossiers as well as excluding "negative words" found in dossiers of technologies with a negative reimbursement decision. Dossiers may be developed in a way that is "more friendly to machine parsing and processing" (p. 28) (Cao et al., 2020). However, whether this strategy would be beneficial will depend on who develop the algorithms and what criteria are used for assessment. Algorithms are open to bias, collusion and manipulation (Cao et al., 2020). It is important that the algorithms that are used are accurate and free from bias, because there is a feedback loop where the outputs further inform algorithms and other analytics (Naughton, 2020). Bias can have implications for reimbursement and costs for patients and the health system (Alami et al., 2020).

Instead of just "deriving insights from data" (p. 5), AI can also be used to evaluate data by determining the quality and assigning a value to datasets, which can be handy to determine what data to prioritize when data are competing or contradicting (Russo & Feng, 2021). Most medication trials compare the active comparator to placebo and it is seldom that high quality trials are conducted that compare interventions head-to-head. To overcome this lack of direct comparison, meta-analysis and network meta-analysis are often conducted to indirectly compare interventions (Salanti, 2012). However, these indirect comparisons are often impossible too, because there is too much heterogeneity. This can be a result of heterogeneity in study populations, definitions, methods, or outcomes between trials. The best way to overcome this is to conduct direct comparison trials where interventions are compared head-to-head. Another way to overcome it is to standardize definitions, outcomes and methods to evaluate and report outcomes. Data wrangling and curation tools may also help with data cleaning and interpretation so it can be combined in a sensible way (Russo & Feng, 2021). Data wrangling consists of several steps such as discovering the data, then structuring, cleaning and validating it, before publishing it (making it assessable for analysis) (TRIFACTA, 2021).

There is a need for HTAs and regulatory processes to be standardized, consistent, transparent and use best practices to improve extraction and interpretation of data, judgement and decision making and reduce bias (Bujar, 2018). Digital technologies and the digital economy can play a positive role in assessing health technologies and making reimbursement decisions. AI can improve access, efficiency and quality in health care (Alami et al., 2020), and it can extract content and is widely used for certain automated financial and reimbursement tasks (Shan, 2020). However, there needs to be effective and transparent collaboration between the several stakeholders involved in a product's life cycle in order to integrate AI effectively as a tool or support system for regulatory and HTA decision-making (Alami et al., 2020). Stakeholders can include HTA agencies, health care professionals, HEOR companies, researchers, patients, payers, regulators, technology- and health technology providers (Alami et al., 2020; Bujar, 2018). These stakeholders must ensure that accurate and appropriate data and sources are used, that a balance is found between added value and uncertainty, that the process and system is constantly evaluated, learned from, and adjustments are made so that AI-related decisions are better informed (Alami et al., 2020). For this to happen, the necessary political, organizational, regulatory and technological conditions for innovation and trust needs to be created (Alami et al., 2020).

Strenghts, limitations and opportunities of digital technologies in healthcare

Data is an asset that can produce revenue, but it's use depends on analytics and infrastructure (Nguyen & Paczos, 2020). "The 3V's of big data [are] volume, variety, velocity" (p. 21), meaning data creates value when it is timely, trustworthy, representative, accessible, and linkable amongst others (Nguyen & Paczos, 2020). A data economy is similar to a digital economy since a digital economy depends on large scale data collection and rapid circulation (Lammi & Pantzar, 2019). In this type of economy, everyone, including citizens, collect and share data (Lammi & Pantzar, 2019). People's behavior can be tracked easily with digital technologies (Goldfarb & Tucker, 2019). In healthcare, this may mean using wearables such as watches that collect objective data such as heart rate, exercise and sleep data (Lammi & Pantzar, 2019), or using apps on smart phones to collect subjective health data through patient-reported outcome questionnaires. This type of data may serve as a motivator to live healthier lives or receive better and more timely health care (European Commission, 2020a). In other words, data can change the way that we behave and make decisions.

With SLRs and HTAs, the digital economy can also be seen from a data and information content and technology perspective (Bukht & Heeks, 2017). Alami et al. conducted an HTA of AI in health care and found that AI can have several clinical, ethical, economic, human, legal, professional and technological implications (Alami et al., 2020). Technological considerations include how AI made decisions and what the decisions are based on (is it free from bias, etc.); clinical considerations include accuracy of recommendations and what is used as the gold/reference standard; human considerations include who is chosen as the target population and who benefits or don't benefit from AI; professional considerations includes how AI impact expertise, skills, training, and timelines; economic considerations include billing and reimbursement biases; and ethical and legal considerations include who is responsible for AI mistakes, what data sources are needed, what privacy concerns are involved, and whether AI should be used as a support tool for decision-making or whether it should be making the decisions (Alami et al., 2020).

There are several limitations with using data and digital technologies in healthcare. Poor data quality can lead to bias and errors in knowledge; technical code (algorithm) flaws could lead to errors in interpretation or inferences regardless of the data quality; criteria for decision-making may not be generalizable or universal; and AI may not be able to adapt to new situations (Alami et al., 2020). If applied on a large scale, defective AI can have a large impact and result in a high cost to the health system or manufacturers and have negative implications for patients (Alami et al., 2020). There is also a concern with regards to cybersecurity and the potential for hacking and tampering (Alami et al., 2020). However, algorithms have been developed to protect the confidentiality and privacy of outsourced medical data (Brumen et al., 2013). In health care, the use of digital technologies to provide digital services is also highly regulated due to privacy issues (UNCTAD, 2019).

Conclusion

This paper has addressed digital technologies that are already used in health care, as well as potential uses for developing and evaluating dossiers for regulatory and HTA agencies. The value of the digital economy depends to a certain extent on the ability to create value from data by transforming data into a product or use it to inform and improve processes, products and efficiency (UNCTAD, 2019). Digital solutions can improve efficiency, optimize resource allocation, and make decision-making more acceptable due to increased transparency (Johnstone et al., 2019). However, there is still a lack of infrastructure to get maximum benefit from all data sources, and there are cybersecurity and privacy concerns, as well as a potential for unintended results (Johnstone et al., 2019). With improvements in digital technology and the digital economy, we may now be moving from digital technology as a support tool towards a reality where we work in human-AI or human-robot teams (Larson & DeChurch, 2020). This may result in a change in human behavior. Implications: Using AI for HTA can save time and allow for the evaluation of large amounts of data. However, it will require high quality data and adequate evaluation of algorithms to ensure it is functioning properly and free from bias and manipulation (Alami et al., 2020).

References and bibliography

1. Aboueid, S., Liu, R., Desta, B., & et al. (2019). The Use of Artificially Intelligent Self-Diagnosing Digital Platforms by the General Public: Scoping Review. JMIR Med Inform, 7(2), e13445. https://doi.org/10.2196/13445
2. Adeva, J. G., Atxa, J. P., Carrillo, M. U., & Zengotitabengoa, E. A. (2014). Automatic text classification to support systematic reviews in medicine. Expert Systems with Applications, 41(4), 1498-1508.
3. Ajam, M., & bookboon.com. (2019). Project Management State of Practice: Current Reality & Filling the Practice Gaps (1st ed.). bookboon.
4. Alami, H., Lehoux, P., Auclair, Y., & et al. (2020). Artificial Intelligence and Health Technology Assessment: Anticipating a New Level of Complexity. J Med Internet Res, 22(7), e17707. https://doi.org/https://doi.org/10.2196/17707

5. Applications of Internet of Things in Healthcare. TheHealthcareInsights. Retrieved May 29 from https://thehealthcareinsights.com/applications-of-internet-of-things-in-healthcare/
6. AWARE. (2021). Biometrics in healthcare: Improved safety and privacy for patients. Retrieved May 29 from https://www.aware.com/blog-biometrics-in-healthcare/
7. Brumen, B., Hericko, M., A, S., & et al. (2013). Outsourcing Medical Data Analyses: Can Technology Overcome Legal, Privacy, and Confidentiality Issues? J Med Internet Res, 15(12), e283. https://doi.org/ 10.2196/jmir.2471
8. Bujar, M. (2018). Development of a Roadmap and Evaluation of Quality Decision-Making Practices during Medicines Development, Regulatory Review and Health Technology Assessment University of Hertfordshire].
9. Bukht, R., & Heeks, R. (2017). Defining, Conceptualising and Measuring the Digital Economy (Development Informatics Working Paper Series, Issue. S. Centre for Development Informatics Global Development Institute.
10. Cao, S., Jiang, W., Yang, B., & Zhang, A. (2020). How to talk when a machine is listening: Corporate disclosure in the age of AI. http:// www.nber.org/papers/w27950
11. European Commission. (2020a). Communication from the Commission to the European Parliament, The Council, The European Economic and Social Committee and The Committee of the Regions: A European strategy for data.
12. European Commission. (2020b). Digital Economy and Society Index (DESI) 2020.
13. European Commission. (2020c). White Paper on Artificial Intelligence - A European approach to excellence and trust. https://ec.europa.eu/info/ sites/default/files/commission-white-paper-artificial-intelligence-feb2020_en.pdf
14. Goldfarb, A., & Tucker, C. (2019). Digital Economics. Journal of Economic LIterature, 57(1), 3-43. https://doi.org/https://doi.org/10.1257/ jel.20171452
15. HIlty, D., Randhawa, K., Maheu, M., & et al. (2020). A Review of

Telepresence, Virtual Reality, and Augmented Reality Applied to Clinical Care. J Technol Behav Sci, 5, 178-205. https://doi.org/https://doi.org/10.1007/s41347-020-00126-x

16. IBM. (2021). Healthcare provider solutions for the modern health system. Retrieved May 25 from https://www.ibm.com/watson-health/ solutions/healthcare-provider

17. ICER. (2018). Guide to Understanding Health Technology Assessment (HTA).

18. Johnstone, N., Agrawala, S., Cornago, E., & et al. (2019). Using Digital Technologies to Improve the Design and Enforcement of Public Policies (OECD Digital Economy Papers, Issue.

19. Khan, S., Mordin, M., Barrows, S., & et al. (2019). PNS169 SIMILARITIES & DIFFERENCES IN GLOBAL VALUE DOSSIER (GVD) AND ACADEMY OF MANAGED CARE PHARMACY (AMCP) DOSSIER DEVELOPMENT. Value in Health, S313.

20. Lammi, M., & Pantzar, M. (2019). The data economy: How technological change has altered the role of the citizen-consumer. Technology in Society. https://doi.org/https://doi.org/10.1016/j.techsoc.2019.101157.

21. Larson, L., & DeChurch, L. (2020). Leading teams in the digital age: Four perspectives on technology and what they mean for leading teams. The Leadership Quarterly, 31, 101377. https://doi.org/https://doi.org/10.1016/j.leaqua.2019.101377

22. Mustonen, E. (2020). Knowledge Sharing in Multinational Virtual Teams Itä-Suomen yliopisto].

23. Naughton, J. (2020, Dec 5). Companies are now writing reports tailored for AI readers – and it should worry us. The Guardian. https://www.theguardian.com/commentisfree/2020/dec/05/companies-are-now-writing-reports-tailored-for-ai-readers-and-it-should-worry-us

24. Nguyen, D., & Paczos, M. (2020). Measuring the Economic Value of Data and Cross-Border Data Flows: A Business Perspective (OECD Digital Economy Papers, Issue.

25. Popoff, E., Besada, M., Jansen, J., & et al. (2020). Aligning text mining and machine learning algorithms with best practices for study selection in

systematic literature reviews. Systematic Reviews, 9, 293. https://doi.org/ https://doi.org/10.1186/s13643-020-01520-5

26. Project Management Institute. (2017). A Guide to the Project Management Body of Knowledge: PMBOK Guide. PMI.

27. Russo, M., & Feng, T. (2021, March 15). The New Tech Tools in Data Sharing. BCG. Retrieved May 8 from https://www.bcg.com/publications/ 2021/new-data-sharing-tools-helping-companies-find-value

28. Salanti, G. (2012). Indirect and mixed-treatment comparison, network, or multiple-treatments meta-analysis: many names, many benefits, many concerns for the next generation evidence synthesis tool. Res Synth Methods, 3(2), 80-97. https://doi.org/10.1002/jrsm.1037

29. Shan, Y. (2020, May 16). How AI Is Transforming Financial Reimbursement. Synced. Retrieved May 26 from https://medium.com/ syncedreview/how-ai-is-transforming-financial-reimbursement-c5d8a1f13978

30. TECHNOSTACKS. (2021). Augmented Reality In Medical Field:Future of AR & Its use cases. Retrieved May 2 from https://technostacks.com/blog/ augmented-reality-in-healthcare

31. TRIFACTA. (2021). Data Wrangling Tools Help Business Save Time. Retrieved May 28 from https://www.trifacta.com/data-wrangling/

32. UNCTAD. (2019). Value creation and capture: Implications for developing countries (978-92-1-112955-7). (Digital Economy Report Issue. U. Nations.

33. Van Der Schouw, M. (2015). Practical Project Management: A User's Guide to Getting Things Done (1st ed.). bookboon.

Contact information

Name of the author: Adinet Lock

Affiliation (University): LIGS University PhD student

Email: adinlock@gmail.com

Appendix I. *Literature Search*

Source	Search Terms	Filters	Results	Included
OECD Library	OECD Digital Economy Papers	Date (2017-present)	49	Nguyen & Paczos 2020; Johnstone et al. 2019
Journal of Medical Internet Research	Digital economy	None	30	Brumen et al. 2013; Aboueid et al. 2019
United Nations	Digital economy	None	1	UNCTAD Report 2019
Technology in Society	Digital economy	None	1	Lammi & Pantzar 2019
Journal of Economic Literature	Digital economy	None	1	Goldfarb & Tucker 2019
BCG	Hand search	None	n/a	Russo & Feng 2021
Google Scholar	"digital economy" AND "medical writing"	Date (2017-present)	12	0
Google Scholar	"artificial intelligence" AND "health technology assessment" AND reimbursement	None	1	Alami et al. 2020
Hand search	N/A	N/A	N/A	Bukht & Heeks 2017; Larson & de Church 2020 Mustonen et al. 2020; TRIFACTA 2021; EC DESI report 2020; EC 2020 White Paper; Shan 2020; Popoff et al. 2020 Bujar 2018; ICER 2018 Khan et al. 2019; Adeva et al. 2014; Naughton 2020; Cao et al. 2020

Source: the Author

Made in the USA
Monee, IL
08 May 2026

49742273R00193